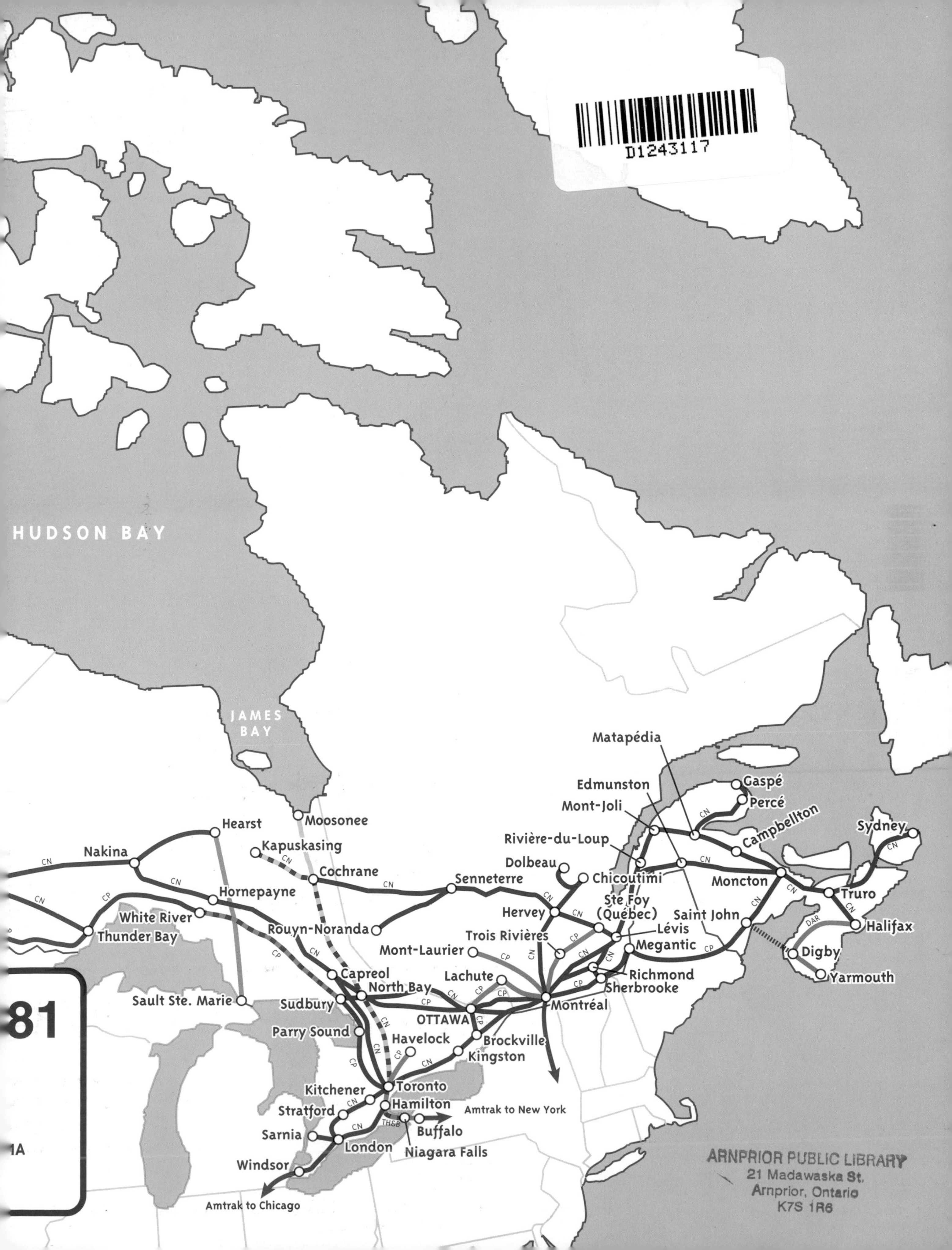
HUDSON BAY
JAMES BAY
Matapédia
Edmunston
Gaspé
Percé
Mont-Joli
Campbellton
Sydney
Rivière-du-Loup
Dolbeau
Chicoutimi
Moncton
Truro
Halifax
Senneterre
Hervey
Ste Foy (Québec)
Saint John
Lévis
Trois Rivières
Megantic
Digby
Yarmouth
DAR
Mont-Laurier
Lachute
Richmond
Sherbrooke
Montréal
Hearst
Moosonee
Kapuskasing
Cochrane
Nakina
Hornepayne
White River
Thunder Bay
Rouyn-Noranda
Capreol
North Bay
Sudbury
Sault Ste. Marie
OTTAWA
Brockville
Kingston
Parry Sound
Havelock
Toronto
Kitchener
Hamilton
Stratford
Amtrak to New York
Sarnia
Buffalo
London
Niagara Falls
TH&B
Windsor
Amtrak to Chicago
CN
CP

fare for all plan

VIA

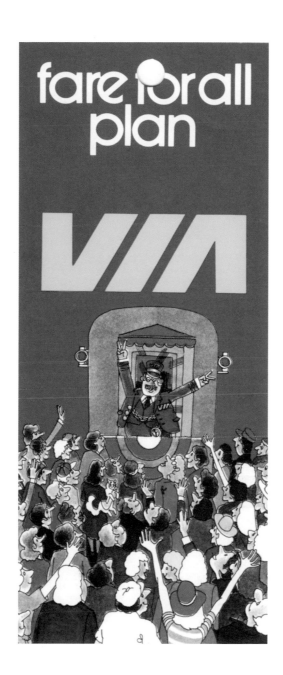

VIA Rail

CHRISTOPHER C.N. GREENLAW

Voyageur Press

Dedication

To my father, Tom, whom I greatly appreciate for bringing me along on countless railway excursions as a little boy. In so doing, you sowed the seeds for the lifelong passion for railroading we share today.

First published in 2007 by Voyageur Press, an imprint of MBI Publishing Company LLC, Galtier Plaza, Suite 200, 380 Jackson Street, St. Paul, MN 55101 USA

Library of Congress Cataloging-in-Publication Data

Greenlaw, Christopher C.N., 1977-
VIA Rail / by Christopher C.N. Greenlaw.
p. cm.
Includes index.
ISBN-13: 978-0-7603-2529-2 (plc w/ jacket)
ISBN-10: 0-7603-2529-4 (plc w/ jacket)
1. VIA Rail Canada. 2. Railroads--Canada. I. Title.
TF27.V47G74 2007
385.0971--dc22

2006029054

Front cover: One of the newest additions to VIA's motive power roster, GE P42DC No. 911 heads up midday train No. 45 just west of Ottawa's Union Station en route to Toronto. *Ian McCord*

Endpapers, front: VIA Rail system map, 1978–1981. *Otto Vondrak*

Back: VIA Rail system map, 1990–2007. *Otto Vondrak*

Frontis: VIA issued this pamphlet in 1979 for its "Fare For All" plan. *Author collection*

Title pages: VIA FP9A No. 6511 leads a three-car consist—train 38—in spring 1989 near the Casselman, Ontario, station. Previously a CN locomotive of the same number, this F unit was later acquired by Algoma Central Railway and renumbered 1752. *A. Ross Harrison*

Back cover: It's July, 27, 1997, and VIA Rail train No. 2, the eastbound *Canadian*, approaches the 1,654-foot (504-meter) Clover Bar Bridge that spans the North Saskatchewan River in Edmonton, Alberta. *Glenn Roemer*

Editor: Dennis Pernu
Designer: Kou Lor

Printed in China

CONTENTS

Acknowledgments

First and foremost, I would like to express my sincerest appreciation to all those who so generously contributed photographic and historical material for the development of this book and will acknowledge each person individually in kind. To my family, I offer my gratitude for their love and support—especially Stacey, who spent an incredible amount of time assisting with the editing process and putting up with both me and this hobby that I enjoy so much. I would like to acknowledge and thank the following people from VIA Rail: Senior Officer of Media and Corporate Communications Catherine Kaloutsky for her assistance, Dave Hunt from the Winnipeg Maintenance Centre, and Service Manager Norma Babineau, along with the entire crew of the eastbound *Ocean* on December 29–30, 2005. I would also like to thank Gail Dever at Canadian National Railway, George de Zwaan and Michael Dufresne from the Library and Archives of Canada, and Marcia Rak from the Canada Museum of Science and Technology. If I happen to be remiss in leaving out anyone, please be assured that my appreciation goes out to you as well.

Heading east on a postcard-perfect winter's day, VIA train No. 2 exits the upper portal of the 2,923-foot (891-meter) Lower Spiral Tunnel carved into the side of Mount Ogden. A triumph of engineering, the Canadian Pacific's Spiral Tunnels were completed in 1909 to reduce the grade of the Big Hill from 4.5 percent to a manageable 2.2 percent and were a sight to behold from the domes of the *Canadian* until its rerouting in 1990. *Andreas Kellar*

INTRODUCTION

The best opportunity for passengers wishing to view the Rocky Mountains in their splendor is aboard the westbound *Canadian* during the summer months. After departing Jasper at around 3:30 in the afternoon, almost six hours of daylight remain to enjoy the scenery. On July 23, 2005, the *Canadian* crosses the truss bridge at Henry House, Alberta, named for the Northwest Company trading fort that once stood near this location and which was abandoned around 1814. *Glenn Roemer*

The story of VIA Rail Canada is one of railroading spiced with political intrigue, which has always been a fundamental component of Canadian railroad history. Since the humble establishment of Canada's first railway on the shores of the Richelieu River in 1836, politics have been intertwined with railway issues by way of consent, land grants, or subsidies.

Financial assistance from the government often proved helpful to the railways, but occasionally, especially during the latter half of the twentieth century, this same benevolent hand was shrouded by meddlesome influence that was occasionally downright destructive. Because of the longstanding relationship between federal subsidy and the railways, the origins of VIA are rooted decades before its conception.

When Canada's rail passenger network was nationalized in the mid-1970s, then–Transport Minister Otto Lang viewed VIA as a "tool of government" with which to make sense of and rationalize a beleaguered passenger train system; his take could not have been more correct. While the VIA "tool" served its purpose for Lang, it also became an entity unto itself that others within government were unwilling to accept.

Use of railway concerns for political gain was by no means a new idea when VIA came along, and because of the way VIA was created, it was left susceptible to the whim of governing powers. As a result, the railway was fashioned into a tool of political opportunism repeatedly used by politicians who cavalierly sacrificed VIA for their own agendas.

Despite the predictions of its detractors and the efforts of certain opponents, VIA Rail Canada has survived. In fact, during the latter half of its 30-year existence, VIA has managed to surpass most expectations and become a successful and essential component of the Canadian passenger transportation system. To understand how VIA has achieved such an accomplishment, we must delve back almost 90 years into the annals of Canadian railway history to examine the factors that led to the Crown Corporation we know today.

The meet between trains 61 and 64 at mile 279 (kilometer 449) of the Kingston Subdivision near Newtonville, Ontario, lasts all of a split-second on a hot day in June 1988. The eight-car consist of train 61, configured in push-pull with LRC-3 6925 in the lead, hurries toward Toronto. In the distance, train 64 disappears into the summer haze. *Andreas Kellar*

CHAPTER ONE

Austere Beginnings: *1919–1967*

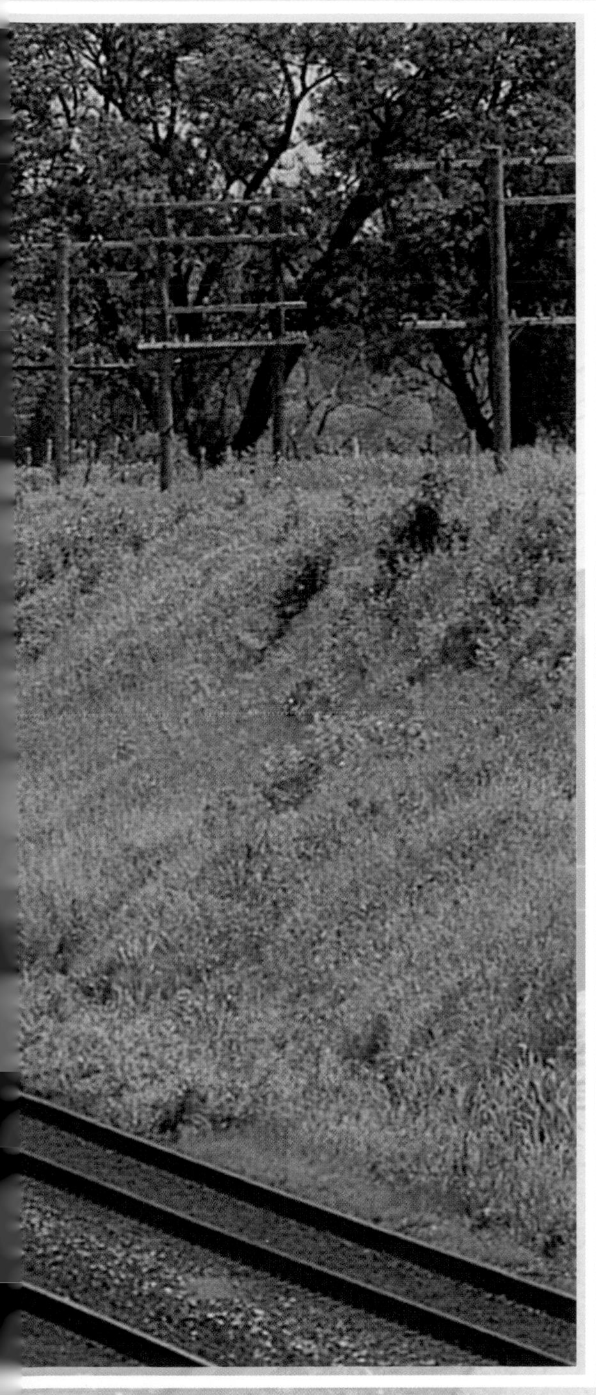

Nationalized rail passenger service in Canada originated during World War I with the inception of the Canadian National Railway (CNR), whose subsequent management of nationwide passenger traffic, equipment, and marketing between 1923 and 1976 created a foundation for the eventual development of VIA Rail. The CNR, as a publicly owned railway, entangled political whim and influence in the fabric

A friendly face amid a driving snowstorm welcomes passengers waiting on the platform, encouraging everyone to hurry along and climb aboard into the warmth of the train. *Coo/West collection*

of Canadian railways and embodied the social and cultural necessity of rail travel for many Canadians.

In 1885 the Canadian Pacific (CPR) completed the first of the three transcontinental railways that would span the Dominion of Canada by the outbreak of World War I in 1914. Inflation and an upsurge in fuel and labor prices prior to and during the war exacerbated the overextension and unmanageable costs of the railways. As a means of solving the financial crises facing rail carriers overburdened with wartime traffic, the Canadian government ordered a Royal Commission on Rail Transport to investigate the consolidation of insolvent railways into a financially stable transportation network capable of competing with the privately owned Canadian Pacific and other foreign roads.

The commission's recommendation was to merge the Canadian Northern, the Grand Trunk, the Canadian Government Railways, and the Intercolonial Railway, along with a series of smaller roads, into a new Crown Corporation that would operate at arm's length from the government, with president, board members, and trustees to be appointed by the presiding federal administration. The merger of these lines began in 1919 with the passing of the Canadian National Railways Act. Designed to be a "marriage between private and public enterprise," the component parts of the new system coalesced in 1923 as the Canadian National Railway Company (CNR).

An interim board overseeing the CNR merger during the spring of 1921 concluded that only growth in the national population would effect an increase in freight tonnage

Already 19 miles (31 kilometers) into their journey to Jonquière, Québec, on January 31, 1992, VIA FP9ARM 6305 and 6308 have yet to leave the island of Montréal. Rather than proceeding north from Central Station through the tunnel beneath Mount Royal, the train takes a clockwise and roundabout route to reach the suburb of Pointe-Aux-Trembles, the last stop on the island before crossing the bridge over the St. Lawrence and continuing northward. *Pierre Ozorák*

and passenger miles for the railways. David Blythe Hanna, the first president of the CNR, did not share this position and formulated a different plan to render the newfound operation profitable. He knew that passenger service was financially counterproductive for the railway, being both service and labor intensive; Hanna was content to let passengers abdicate his rails for the CPR. Significant friction during the fall and winter of 1921 between Hanna and the point man for his employer, newly elected Prime Minister Mackenzie King, prevented such an occurrence. The discord between the two men led to Hanna's resignation, and Mackenzie King appointed Sir Henry Thornton president of the CNR on October 10, 1922.

Sir Henry Thornton

Despite the financial burden that passenger travel placed on a railway, Thornton appreciated the need for rail passenger service in Canada, and his credentials for managing passenger service were extensive. As general superintendent of the commuter-centered Long Island Rail Road in 1901, Thornton oversaw the daily flood of trains through Manhattan's Penn Station. Knowledge and experience gained in the United States served him well overseas throughout World War I, where he was recruited to speed up troop movements in England and France for the British government, which had nationalized their railways for the duration of the war. Prior to his arrival in Canada during the summer of 1922, Thornton (knighted for his wartime efforts) was instrumental in revitalizing commuter service for the Great Eastern Railway in the United Kingdom, and was well prepared to take the helm of the publicly owned CNR. In fact, his latest achievement in transforming the busiest

Inbound and outbound. With the Halifax terminal almost in sight, VIA train No. 14, the *Ocean*, passes a three-car set of RDC-1s that has just departed for Truro and Sydney, Nova Scotia, on September 5, 1988. Halifax–Sydney service has only one year and four months left before being discontinued on January 15, 1990. *James C. Herold photo, author collection*

commuter line in the world from "one of the worst to one of the most [efficient]" had much to do with Thornton's appointment to the CNR. Thornton's tenure lasted throughout the Roaring '20s until the onset of the Great Depression. During his term, the CNR acquired a fleet of passenger equipment and implemented a service structure that outlasted the halcyon days of the passenger train into the 1950s.

Thornton foresaw the impending threat automobiles posed to rail passenger service and steered the CNR to attack the problem head-on, attempting to entice passengers back to the rails. Unlike his predecessor's freight-centered approach to solvency and profit, Thornton vied for passengers. Notwithstanding the costs associated with such ventures, intense competition ensued between the CNR and rival CPR to capture the attention of the traveling public throughout the 1920s. The result was comfortable, European-styled service, among the finest available in North America. Transcontinental trains on both railroads were soon noted more for lavish comfort than expeditious schedules.

In contrast to the transcontinental service and in keeping with Sir Henry's focus on the CNR as "The People's Road," reasonably priced, high-speed intercity service was inaugurated on certain routes departing from points between the cities of Québec City, Québec, and Windsor, Ontario, a rail corridor that would become the most profitable region of rail service in Canada. Trains such as the Toronto–Ottawa *Capital City* and the *Queen City* between Montréal and Québec City were faster, affordable, and adequately comfortable, trumping their rivals on the CPR. This infuriated CPR President Sir Edward Beatty who, already disdainful of Crown enterprise, claimed that Thornton was nothing more than a showman aspiring to render the CPR to "a condition of inferiority . . . [by duplicating and] surpassing every facility furnished by the Canadian Pacific."

Regardless, the Canadian National continued to innovate and modernize its services. Under Thornton, the CNR acquired 20 percent more passenger equipment than its rival, amassing a more modern fleet in an attempt to surpass the amenities and services provided on the CPR's *Trans-Canada Limited*. The CNR contemporized its passenger roster to include innovations such as onboard shower facilities and added a variety of other services such as exercise spaces and choice of accommodations, including both single and double bedrooms. More impressive were the lounge cars equipped with barbershops, soda fountains, and a system of two-way telephones. The first network radio was broadcast from a CNR train in 1923, and five years later Canada's first road diesel was placed into passenger service, covering the distance between Montréal and Toronto in an unprecedented 7 hours and 40 minutes at speeds up to 80 miles (129 kilometers) per hour. Unfortunately, the stock market crash in 1929 would bring the increasingly luxurious service on both railways to a grinding halt. The future of passenger rail travel in Canada would again be in peril.

Duff Commission and Pooling of Service

In 1932, a second Royal Commission on Rail Transport was convened under Chief Justice Lyman Poore Duff. Duff held little regard for those who engaged in lavish spending of public money and his sentiment was shared by numerous parliamentarians from the ruling Conservative party. Believing that Thornton sought immunity from governmental control and influence, the Conservatives formed a coalition intent on sacking him for what they understood to be mismanagement for the sake of wasteful display. Thornton's career as the head of CNR was on borrowed time.

Pressure mounted as the anti-Thornton camp issued a six-page memorandum favoring the dismissal of the CNR president. Worse, Duff's investigation into Thornton and CNR management claimed that a "red thread of extravagance ran through [Thornton's] managerial staff." Thornton felt as though he had lost the confidence of the Canadian people and fearing that the findings of the Duff Commission were potentially damaging, resigned prior to the release of the report.

Despite Thornton's resignation, the revision of the Railway Act that eventually incorporated the findings of the Duff Commission included a separate piece of legislation designed specifically to curtail the fierce competitive struggle between the railways and their presidents, believed to be the root cause of overspending and financial duress. Under the Canadian National–Canadian Pacific Act of 1933, the railways were required to pool certain passenger services in the Québec City–Windsor Corridor. Subsequently, a contrasting assortment of liveries on pooled passenger trains were a common sight across Ontario and Québec until the mid-1960s. Pooling of transcontinental passenger traffic was also discussed but never implemented due to continual bickering between the railways over which station to use in Montréal.

The changes the Duff Commission initiated succeeded in establishing an equitable balance of power for intercity passenger services on both roads. Coupled with the economic downturn of the 1930s, the competitive train-for-train spending frenzy came to an end.

Cause and Effect

By the middle of the twentieth century, the sizeable armada of heavyweight and semi-streamlined passenger equipment on both the Canadian National and Canadian Pacific had endured two long yet drastically different decades of service. The opulent service that

It's Christmas Day 1986 in the Land of Evangeline. VIA RDC-1 No. 6119 and sister stop in front of the historic VIA station in Kentville, Nova Scotia, that once served as the headquarters for the Dominion Atlantic Railway. Note the wreath placed inside the forward diaphragm on 6119. *Coo/West collection*

once adorned most rolling stock had long since been replaced by more functional revenue-generating equipment. The hardship of the Great Depression and the corresponding drop in demand for passenger service throughout the 1930s resulted in a large quantity of rail equipment sitting stagnant in coach yards across the Dominion. In contrast, the heavy demand on railway equipment and increased traffic a mere decade later during World War II stretched the capabilities of the railways to their limits.

The postwar years differed much from the 1920s and 1930s as the Canadian public envisioned a brighter future replete with jobs, increased salaries, and time for relaxation. Travelers began to look once more toward the rails for holiday and business travel, and the railways coped with this influx by replacing and modernizing their war-weary passenger equipment. Changing tastes of a public that increasingly preferred automobile and airline travel would force a reexamination of this investment, although much after the fact.

The 1950s were difficult times for railway management due to the downturn on rail traffic in favor of air and truck transport and the inability of industry leaders to foresee the future. For many railways in the United States, the prospect of a return to gainful and prosperous freight traffic was bleak. In an attempt to recover lost freight service and mounting financial losses, scores of unprofitable passenger runs were discontinued and what remained of a once vibrant passenger network was increasingly neglected. Some of the larger U.S. railways made attempts to woo the traveling public back through the modernization of several well-known name trains, but they avoided the purchase of new passenger equipment wherever possible. North of the border, however, things were quite different for passenger trains.

Although the downturn in rail traffic was just as evident in Canada, federal statutes that regulated the price of rail travel—a different approach to governing the transportation industry—mitigated the impact of declining ridership for a period. Passenger services on the CNR and CPR did not immediately suffer the same fate as those in the United States, and both of Canada's trans-national railways attempted a renaissance of rail travel throughout the early 1950s. In fact, the CNR's rejuvenation profited

greatly from a readily available surplus of American passenger equipment.

Railway presidents Donald Gordon and Norris Roy "Buck" Crump of the CNR and CPR, respectively, also held the potential for passenger service in higher esteem than their American counterparts. In an interview with the late Norman de Poe that appeared in *Saturday Night* magazine, both men scoffed at the ominous prediction of then–Interstate Commerce Commissioner Howard Hosner that North America would see the end of rail passenger service by 1970. While in agreement about the potential for the passenger train in Canada, each president set about their attempts at revitalization quite differently and the choices they made throughout the 1950s and 1960s would set the stage for a nationalized rail passenger system and equip VIA Rail into the next millennium.

Norris Roy "Buck" Crump and the CPR's Stainless-Steel *Canadian*

Aside from a few modernized heavyweight cars and a complement of modern, smooth-sided lightweight passenger cars, the bulk of the CPR passenger fleet in the early 1950s consisted of older steel-framed heavyweight equipment that was worn out from wartime service. The automobile and availability of air travel resulted in a significant decline in passenger traffic between 1945 and 1952 from 50.6 million riders per year to 29.9 million. Under Crump's direction, the CPR would make one final attempt at revitalizing its flagging passenger service.

Crump began his career with the CPR as a railway laborer before establishing himself as a member of the company's executive corps. He knew the railway business from the ground up. Using that extensive knowledge, he focused his attention on reviving the slump in passenger service. Crump believed that the problem of diminishing railway

Until 1970, at least five U.S. railways offered service to Canadian cities. The Great Northern had a morning and afternoon edition of the *International* from Seattle to Vancouver, as well as the *Winnipeg Limited* which ran to that city from St. Paul, Minnesota. The Grand Trunk Western's *Maple Leaf* and *International Limited* served Toronto from New York and Chicago, respectively. Travelers to Montréal could ride aboard the Delaware & Hudson's *Laurentian* or *Montreal Limited* from New York or choose the Boston & Maine's *Montrealer* or *Ambassador* from either Washington, D.C., or New York. By the mid-1980s, only a few of these trains remained. VIA and Amtrak revived the *International* and operated it jointly until 2004. Here, Amtrak F40PH leads this train near Dundas, Ontario, on January 18, 1987, with a mixed consist of six Amfleet cars and three of VIA's *Tempo* coaches. *Andreas Kellar*

CANADIAN
NATIONAL
RAILWAYS
Serves all 10
provinces of Canada
and 12 states in U.S.A.

Perhaps the finest livery ever adopted by CN, the olive green, black, and gold color scheme was also short-lived. Here it is shown on a ticket sleeve from 1959. *Author collection*

passenger travel on the CPR was not only the availability of other transportation modes but also outdated equipment and service. The panacea to the passenger problem, he believed, began with the refurbishment of the existing fleet and the addition of a new transcontinental train composed of modern, streamlined equipment. Crump began by forming a committee to examine the issue and to oversee the purchase of new equipment.

In revitalizing CPR passenger service, Crump applied the same hands-on, walkabout approach for which he was known throughout his career. His desire to understand the needs of the passenger led to his personal examination of equipment already in service across North America. Crump and his committee traveled on numerous name trains such as the Great Northern's *Empire Builder* and the New York Central's *20th Century Limited.* Crump was most impressed with the *California Zephyr* and its stainless-steel consist, overall performance, and exemplary service. It was decided that the CPR's new name train and streamlined fleet would be modeled after the famous *Zephyr* and christened *The Canadian.*

Built by the Budd Company of Philadelphia, Pennsylvania, the stainless-steel equipment used on the *Zephyrs* was both lightweight and inexpensive to maintain—two features that were essential for revitalizing a cost-intensive service. In preparation for the inauguration of *The Canadian* the following year, and for use on other trains around the system, an order for 173 cars was placed with the Budd Company in 1954. The fleet was divided into seven different car types that formed 15 complete train sets and included Canada's first transcontinental dome cars.

On April 24, 1955, amid great fanfare, Crump (appointed president of the CPR by its board members some months prior to this ceremony) was on hand at Windsor Station in Montréal for the inaugural send-off of *The Canadian.* The train and its 2,881-mile (4,637-kilometer) route to Vancouver, British Columbia, were an instant

1229
8516
8516
CP Rail
8516
8513
8513
CP Rail

success and remained so throughout its inaugural year. Crump was pleased, commenting on "his" train to a *Montreal Gazette* reporter by stating that "she's a beauty." He mocked the fledgling airline industry, at the time plagued with poor serviceability and delays, by joking, "If you've got time to spare, go by air."

Despite Crump's support for *The Canadian*, by the end of the year he came to understand that it was not the solution he had anticipated. Changing trends in the passenger transportation industry revealed that the airlines he so cavalierly mocked would inevitably have the last word. A man of utilitarian mindset, Crump placed the needs of the company before public sentimentality. Under Crump's business-oriented leadership, the CPR would follow the example of American railroads and move away from passenger services.

Some 20 years later, on the eve of the nationalized passenger service that would become VIA Rail, Crump unremorsefully reflected on his mid-1950s attempt at revitalization by saying that it had been a mistake that was not financially viable, and that no justification existed for rail passenger service in Canada. "I gave it a try in 1955 when we put *The Canadian* in service," he stated. "[However, it] was too late. The public left us. It took 123 damned employees to run from Montréal to Vancouver and we couldn't charge rates commensurate to pay the expenses." By the fall of 1955, Crump committed to curtail passenger service and by the end of the decade, more than 50 trains were reduced in service or eliminated altogether.

The noncorrosive stainless-steel fleet of the 1955 *Canadian* could not have been a better choice. Although it was not the first stainless-steel streamliner to ply Canadian rails (the CPR having been trumped by the New York Central's *Empire State Express* some 12 1/2 years earlier), the unique "shotweld" construction technique developed by Budd

CP Rail motive power and red-striped equipment give little indication that the *Canadian* is indeed a VIA train on July 15, 1979. As the train approaches the Great Divide, steam generator–equipped GP9s 8516, 8513, and 8517, along with F9B No. 1964, lead train No. 1 into Stephen, British Columbia, for a pending meet with a westbound freight. *Richard Yaremko*

Adorned in her original 1950s livery of grey and Tuscan red, Canadian Pacific FP7 No. 1428 leads a 12-car consist of *The Canadian* through Lachine, Québec. *Author collection*

yielded a formidable product that railroads across North America learned to rely on. Thus, the choice to equip *The Canadian* with stainless steel resulted in a roster of equipment that would endure to eventually serve VIA Rail passengers. Not to be outdone, the CNR had also launched an impressive transcontinental the same day as *The Canadian*.

Donald Gordon and the *Super Continental*

During the postwar years, the Canadian National faced the same conditions of degenerating equipment and declining revenues as the CPR and also took steps in the early 1950s to refurbish their passenger car fleet, launching their own streamlined transcontinental. However, unlike the CPR, the Canadian National's effort to revitalize passenger service would persist well into the 1960s and their expenditures on new equipment would be the largest one-time order of cars ever placed by a North American railroad.

Donald Gordon was appointed as CNR president in 1950 and brought with him a people-oriented approach to management and passenger service that harkened

The Canadian Pacific travel system truly did "Span the World" in the 1950s. This ticket sleeve was issued for travel on the CPR's *Dominion* from Vancouver to Toronto on June 17, 1954. *Author collection*

A pair of cab units led by CP Rail FP9 No. 1411 pause with *The Canadian* in tow at White River, Ontario, in July 1978. As part of the CP's contribution of equipment to the joint CN-CP *Centennial Train* in 1967, No. 1411 donned a special livery and was renumbered 1867, the year of Canada's founding. *W. H. Coo, Coo/West collection*

back to the days of Sir Henry Thornton. Gordon shared Thornton's view of the passenger train as the most visible and least lucrative aspect of railroading, but unlike Thornton, Gordon had no desire to resume the fierce competition that once existed between the CNR and CPR.

For Gordon, the future of passenger service was uncertain. "It had become a fine question whether people were abandoning the railways or the railways were abandoning the people," he said, "but to lure them back with faster trains and reliable service would need tremendous capital investment." Gordon was reluctant to devote funds to a service whose ridership continued to decrease, but the federal government, backed by a constituency that romanticized rail travel, prevented any reduction in service. Invariably, the legislated requirement of the railway to provide passenger service, along with political pressure to adhere with this mandate, won the day, and the CNR chose to revitalize the passenger train in a manner that was sensible, affordable, and comfortable. "We chose to be practical," Gordon said, "to obtain as much new, modern equipment as we could get for our money and spread it throughout the Canadian National Railway System for the benefit of as many travelers as possible."

In anticipation of the 1955 launch of their *Super Continental*, the CNR learned that it would require a substantial fleet of modern rolling stock to equip not only its flagship train, but also other routes around the network. Thus, the CNR was forced by government mandate to provide national rail passenger service to extend their equipment purchase far beyond the dozen or so train sets needed for daily transcontinental service. In 1950 the CNR placed an order with Canadian Car and Foundry (CC&F) for 218 first-class

With towering thunderstorm clouds in the background, the westbound *Super Continental* makes its crew change at Edson, Alberta, in August 1977. *Richard Yaremko*

coaches to form the backbone of their contemporary passenger fleet, as well as 20 sleeping cars with a unique 24–duplex roomette configuration, purchased in an attempt to appeal to the thrifty business traveler. Pullman Standard was contracted to build 141 sleeping, dining, and parlor cars in no less than 8 different configurations, including 52 E-series sleeping cars that provided an assortment of affordable accommodations to attract passengers to overnight travel. It was an unprecedented move that stunned the industry; at a time when rail passenger service faced an obvious downturn, the CNR equipment order totaled 359 new cars and cost in excess of $60 million.

CNR also re-shopped their heavyweight fleet, modernizing and refurbishing an assortment of sleeping and parlor cars. To ensure that this older equipment adequately matched their new acquisitions, a "streamstyled" design was applied to the old heavyweight cars that included a contoured cover over their clerestory roofs and gallery windows.

Though often overshadowed in the eye of the railway romantic by the streamlined *Canadian*'s gleaming stainless-steel consist, the *Super Continental* was inaugurated on April 24, 1955. The new and modernized equipment in its attractive olive green and black livery, highlighted by gold pinstripes and complemented with a maple leaf roundel at the side ends of each car, was a stunning sight that appealed to the traveling public, but it was only the beginning.

Pierre Delagrave: The Grandfather of VIA Rail

By the late 1950s, with ridership beginning to wane on Canadian rails, regulatory issues concerning freight tariffs and increasing competition with the trucking industry stymied Donald Gordon's attempts to ensure the railway's profitability and solvency. The same regulatory forces that required the maintenance of passenger service on the CNR during the early part of the decade maintained the status quo, although financial losses continued to escalate. If Gordon were to keep the passenger train alive on the CNR, he would have to find his own solution.

Mounting social and political upheaval between French and English Canada was also of significant interest to Canada's largest Crown Corporation. In partial response to an ever-increasing requirement for representation of francophone employees among executive circles within CNR, Donald Gordon

Rounding the curve at Shepard, Alberta, on September 15, 1979, VIA FP9A 1410 and RS-10 8558 lead the eastbound *Canadian* along the CP's Brooks Subdivision to Medicine Hat. The long-end-forward orientation of the Skyline dome seen here changed in 1982 after VIA modified this equipment. The buffet seating under the dome was removed to permit the installation of a snack bar, and all 26 coach seats situated in the long end of the car were supplanted with six tables to seat or dine 12 patrons. Without the need to mate the coach section of the Skylines with the 100-series coaches, the dome cars were turned around to run short end first, allowing the dining area to function either as seating for the galley underneath the dome or as overflow seating for a dining car, if required. *Richard Yaremko*

Since its inaugural run on June 3, 1904, the *Ocean* has changed owners three times and survived more than 100 years of politics and service cuts to become North America's longest-running regularly scheduled name train. Most likely taken in the Matapédia River Valley of northern New Brunswick sometime between 1978 and 1982, this photograph of VIA FPA-4 6788 and FPB-4 6852 at the head end of a 10-car consist of the *Ocean* was used by VIA for press releases and newspaper publicity photos. However, when published in newspapers, the brilliant colors provided by the autumn foliage and the clean, sleek blue and yellow of the *Ocean* were never as crisp or vivid as they are here. *VIA photo, Coo/West collection*

appointed Pierre Delagrave, although not merely because of his cultural and linguistic roots. His tenures first as sales manager then as vice-president of passenger services demonstrated that he saw the passenger train as a potentially profitable enterprise, based on better service, cheaper fares, and better equipment. Delagrave's personal notes, now preserved at the Library and Archives of Canada, reveal a macro-understanding of the benefits of a well-run passenger service. The quality of passenger service, he wrote, leads people to "decide what type of company we are . . . if a businessman aboard our trains receives good customer service, he'd get the feeling that his freight would [be treated] the same way."

Delagrave's most pressing concern was the need to educate passenger train crews in customer service. Since crew departments functioned independently, there was a disconnect between the Passenger Department, which was responsible for passenger comfort and customer service, and the Operating Department, responsible for onboard service crews. Hiring practices that favored seniority over demonstrated service ability meant that crewmembers were often ill-equipped for their jobs. As Delagrave explained, "There were conductors and stewards who had no [formal] training in service and public relations, men who knew only the operation of trains. I sat in the dining car for dinner once and asked for a glass of wine and got a glass of vermouth! It wasn't their fault—they had not been taught. So we made a booklet to explain everything, wines and so on, and gave three-day classes."

Delagrave initiated appropriate customer-service training programs for all frontline staff members and pressed Donald Gordon to abolish the practice of seniority-based recruitment of passenger service personnel. The process met with resistance from those who insisted that there was no other way of doing business and who were more concerned with their seniority than with the company's prospects. One story of his effort to improve employee attitudes recounts Delagrave traveling on the overnight train between Montréal and Toronto, to be woken up halfway by an excessively rough ride. During a stopover in Brockville, Ontario, Delagrave donned his housecoat and stormed down the platform toward the locomotive. Confronting the engineer climbing out of the locomotive, Delagrave thrust out his hand to introduce himself saying, "It's my job to get people on these trains. I just want to tell you that if you keep driving the way you did tonight, I'm wasting my time."

"The Only Cheaper Way to Travel Is Walking"

Next, Pierre Delagrave turned his attention to fares and scheduling, discovering that more than 50 different fares existed for travel between Montréal and Toronto and that price varied inversely with the busiest travel times. CNR transportation economist Garth Campbell assisted in developing the solution: an entirely new fare structure that varied according to the degree of demand, with prices differentiated on the basis of high, medium, and low periods of travel. In order to simplify advertisement and public understanding, Delagrave wanted to apply a simple yet effective title to the concept. "We wanted to give it a catchy name, and one night in the *Montreal Star*, Eaton's [department store] was advertising a 'red, white and blue sale', whatever that meant, but it sounded catchy and that's how the name of our Red, White and Blue fare plan was born."

The idea was simple yet ingenious: Red, or bargain fares, were offered on the 160 lightest travel days of the year; White economy fares were applied during the 140 days of increased travel throughout the warmer months; and Blue fares covered the 60 days of holiday and vacation travel when passenger traffic was at its peak. The new fare structure was instituted on May 1, 1962, as part of a pilot project on the *Ocean* between Montréal and Halifax with the slogan, "The only cheaper way to travel is walking." The effort was so successful—increasing ridership by 46 percent—that it was phased in throughout the entire system by May 1964.

Voices of Opposition

Government subsidy of the railways is a traditional source of discord within the Canadian transportation industry that has set the railways against a variety of shippers ever since the building of the Canadian Pacific. When Crump and Gordon signed an agreement with the government to receive funding geared

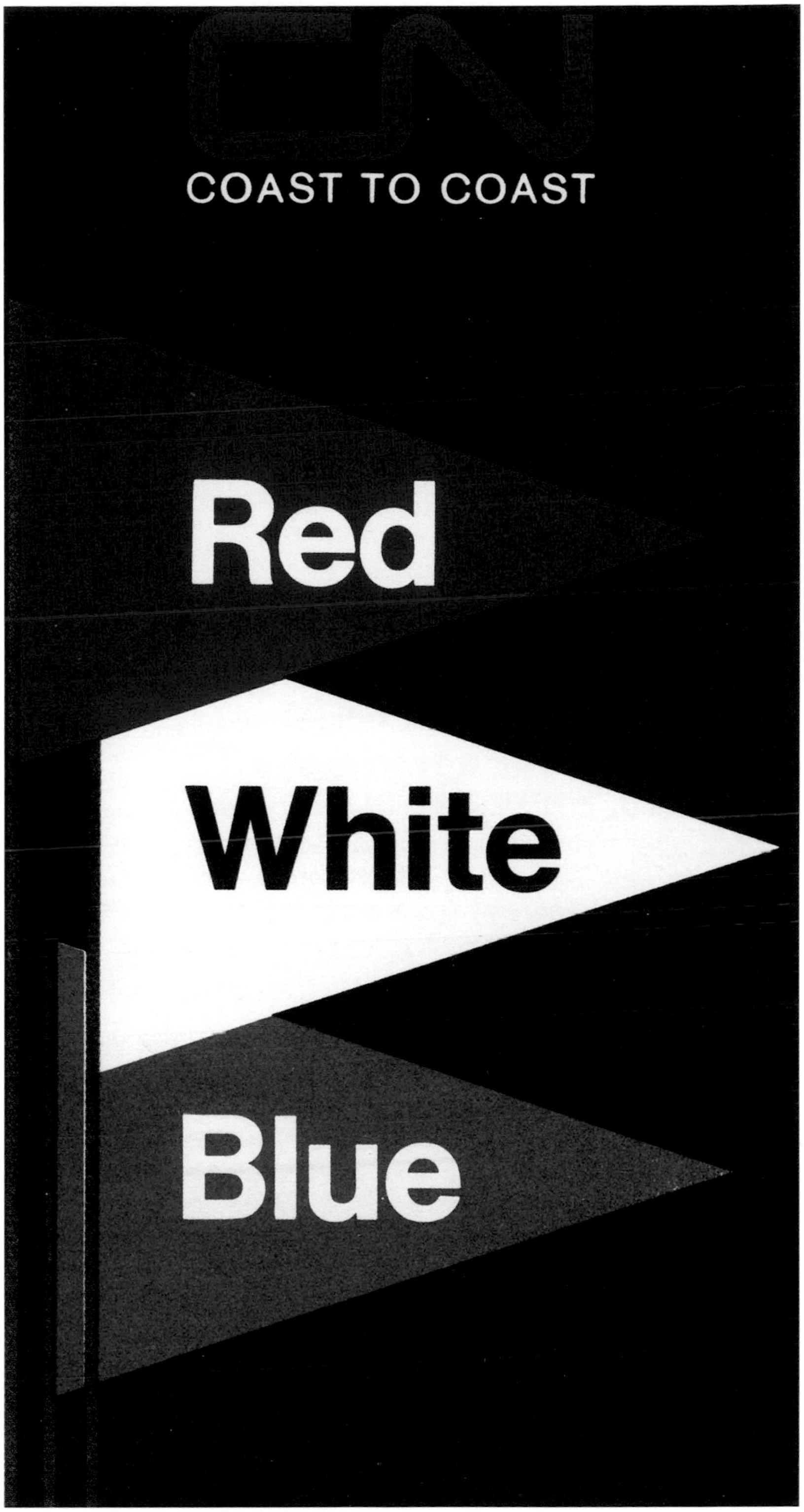

This Canadian National "Red, White and Blue" brochure dated October 1, 1969, through September 30, 1970, contains fare information for CN lines in Canada and for Grand Trunk Western lines in the United States. One-way coach fare from Halifax to Vancouver cost only $66. *Author collection*

Since 1955, RDCs have handled the passenger services on Vancouver Island, which today remains one of the last two bastions of regular RDC operation in North America. One attraction of the island run is the spectacular bridge over Niagara Creek. This 529-foot steel trestle was fabricated in England in 1883, shipped to Port Moody in pieces, and reassembled at Cisco, British Columbia, for the completion of the first Canadian transcontinental railway. Around 1910 it was disassembled and moved to this site, replacing an earlier, aging timber trestle. Here, the *Malahat* creeps carefully across the 260-foot-high deck on May 26, 1986. Speed is reduced on this crossing where the view downward is short but always breathtaking.
Robert Sandusky

specifically for passenger services for the first time in 1962, a seemingly ritualistic series of complaints from the budding intercity bus industry became an almost annual event.

The Red, White and Blue fare plan attracted customers back to the rails and garnered significant growth in passenger miles for CNR, but it also had the undesired effect of strengthening the ever-growing voice of opposition against subsidized and publicly owned rail passenger services in Canada. The notion that the CNR should desire to be competitive and yield dividends for its shareholders, the Canadian taxpayers, became a point of disgust and a rallying call against the continuation of passenger trains.

Rail passenger detractors were initially led by the Canadian Motor Coach Association, which lamented that the Red, White and Blue fare structure was inherently unjust, undercutting fares offered by other modes of transport. In the opinion of rail opponents, governmental funding covered or absorbed losses the railways sustained, whereas buses, for example, enjoyed no subsidization whatsoever. Mounting dissent by the Motor Coach Association and its affiliates resulted in the summoning of CNR Presi-

The wooden Canadian Pacific station at Dorval, Québec, stood for almost a century on this location before being closed in 1984 and razed some time later. In January 1979, the westbound *Super Continental* will pass by the platform. After entraining passengers at the VIA station located across the adjacent CN tracks, VIA FP9 No. 6519, still in CN paint, backed the *Super* along the CN-CP crossover track, laid in place initially for pool train service, in order to continue on to Ottawa by way of CP's M&O Subdivision. *Author collection*

dent Donald Gordon before members of Parliament in Ottawa where he was forced to justify the railway's efforts to lure back the traveling public.

Unfortunately for the publicly owned railway, industry resistance would continue to plague each endeavor to increase passenger sales. The introduction of Car-Go-Rail service in June 1963 drew heavy criticism from car rental agencies across Canada, which complained of decreasing rental sales due to passengers shipping their personal vehicles by rail to their destinations of choice.

The MacPherson Commission

A fourth Royal Commission on Rail Transport was convened in the early 1960s to address freight service issues. Incidental to the MacPherson Commission agenda was concern from the railways over their losses in passenger revenues. The CNR and CPR plead their respective cases to the commission, requesting a change in freight rates and a solution to mounting passenger service debt, citing operating losses of more than $50 million and $40 million, respectively, in years leading up 1960. Where the two railroads differed was in their specific approaches to service provision and the 1933 pool train arrangement.

The CPR wanted to curtail its passenger service but felt restricted. In a submission to the MacPherson Commission in 1959, the CPR expressed displeasure at operating passenger trains under federal mandates such as the pooling arrangement. The railway believed that commensurate fares were necessary to operate such "required" services, but was loath to charge them to each passenger. Essentially, the CPR wanted to be either subsidized or permitted to abandon passenger operations altogether. The CNR, on the other hand, desired to continue its expansion and improvement of passenger services.

When the commission finally tabled its report in March 1961, it recognized that passenger service was clearly an unprofitable aspect of rail operations that had become "obsolete." The report also concluded that if the federal government continued to mandate that the railways provide rail passenger service under the auspices of public interest, then subsidization of such services was necessary.

Federal politics during the period of the MacPherson Commission had much to do with the timing of the implementation of its recommendations. In the Canadian political system, an elected minority government does not hold enough sway over Parliament to enact any one finding into law unopposed. The government would remain in such a state until the latter part of the 1960s when a majority government was finally elected and legislation of the National Transportation Act in 1967 permitted the necessary changes. All the same, those concerned with decision making for the provision of passenger services knew full well that it was only a matter of time before the recommendations of the MacPherson Report were adopted, so the CNR and CPR furthered their respective agendas in anticipation of the new law.

At the CNR, Delagrave wasted little time taking advantage of the momentum gained by the railway's new fare structure and ever-increasing ridership by reexamining service in the most profitable sector of Canadian rail travel: the Québec City–Windsor Corridor. Delagrave continued to diversify the roster and incorporate additional onboard services. In order to further invigorate passenger travel on the CNR, he decided to capitalize on the availability of surplus rolling stock in the United States resulting from numerous discontinued trains there.

Rebirth Following the End of Pool Trains

Throughout the early 1960s, the CNR remarkably continued to draw travelers back to the rails, and revenues increased for the first time since World War II. The CNR embarked on a second rejuvenation that began with a transformation of their corporate image and trademark. The familiar Canadian National maple leaf and waferboard herald was replaced with a simplified, futuristic logo that combined the C and the N into a single distinctive, freeform figure. By dropping the R to render the design fully bilingual, the logo created by Allan R. Fleming of Toronto represented the fluid movement of people, material, and messages throughout the country. The tri-tone color scheme applied to locomotives and cars of the *Super Continental* in 1955 was exchanged for a crisp, two-tone black and light-gray (almost white) livery; this fresh look was the wave of the future for CN, appropriate for a decade that appeared full of promise.

The CN made their first acquisition of surplus U.S. equipment in 1963 in the form of a five-car stainless-steel streamliner from the Reading Railroad. Refurbished with a modern Euro-styled interior and rechristened *Le Champlain*, the former Budd-built equipment was pressed into service between Montréal and Québec City, shaving a full half-hour off the schedule. The new *Champlain*, along with six "Skytop" observation lounge/sleeping cars purchased from The Milwaukee Road and rechristened as "Skyview" lounges on the daily Montréal–Halifax *Ocean*, provided a traveling experience unique to CN.

Although Delagrave continued to formulate new ideas for service in the Corridor, the 30-year-old pool train agreement between the CN and CPR was a formidable barrier to a revamped schedule. Under this mandated and inflexible arrangement, passengers could opt for one of only three departures between Montréal and Toronto each day. Any schedule modification that Delagrave wished to make required a long and tedious process and the subsequent agreement of the CPR. To enable innovation and make the most of a highly traveled and populated rail corridor, the pool system had to go.

Dissolution of the pool agreement illustrates the diverging philosophies of senior railway executives in Canada. When approached by the CN to discontinue their agreement, the CPR obliged. In fact, resentment toward the agreement was growing among CPR executives forced to sustain passenger services at a loss. CPR President Buck Crump even admitted publicly in 1965 that he intended to drop transcontinental service as soon as possible. This admission resulted in a flood of indignation from Canadians, some claiming that should the CPR ever terminate passenger service,

In addition to the Montréal–Saint John–Halifax *Atlantic*, VIA offered daily local service over the Halifax–Moncton–Saint John portion of this route. A single RDC-1 approaches the quaint wood-framed station at Petitcodiac, New Brunswick, during the summer of 1988. *Coo/West collection*

they ought to repatriate the land grants assigned to the railway in the late 1800s. Perhaps for this reason alone, the Canadian Pacific ran the shortest-lived name train in Canadian railway history.

The joint passenger pool was abolished on October 30, 1965, and on the same day that Pierre Delagrave put his plan for renaissance into action, the CPR replied with a move contradictory to their claimed disdain for passenger service. As if to pay lip service to pundits, the introduction of the *Chateau Champlain*/*Royal York*, whose name changed depending on direction of travel, coincided with the end of the pooling arrangement. The consist mirrored that of *The Canadian*, minus the sleeping cars, and provided service between Toronto and Montréal in a reasonable 5 hours and 45 minutes. Sadly, this confusing gambit was nothing more than a flailing last stab in the Corridor—the elimination of the *Royal York* from the CPR timetable came less than three months after its introduction. The train rolled the last revenue miles of its brief life with only a score of passengers to bear witness to what would soon become only an afterthought in Canadian railway history. Things were very different at CN.

The Fastest Intercity Service in North America

Claiming that the rapid intercity service proposed by Delagrave was impossible, Canadian National's Operating Department, with support from equipment personnel, stonewalled any such innovation on the railway. Undaunted, Delagrave approached Gordon, detailing that the efficiency of passenger service in the Corridor was no different than it had been during the days of Sir Henry Thornton more than 35 years earlier. Gordon threw his support behind Delagrave, and the elimination of the restrictive pool train agreement removed the last remaining barrier to faster and improved service in the Corridor.

Amid gala ceremonies in Toronto and Montréal, CN train sets lettered for the new higher-speed *Rapido* service were unveiled. The concept was simple: use conventional equipment and improve scheduling. At 4:45 p.m. daily, except Saturday, nonstop *Rapido* trains left both major centers, making the 335-mile (539-kilometer) trip in less than five hours, a full hour and a quarter faster than the previous pool schedule and the fastest intercity service in all of North America.

Rapido trains were an instant success and Delagrave continued to broaden the scope of expedited rail travel by adding three more

Among the varied collection of rolling stock that VIA inherited were the cars that introduced Budd stainless-steel equipment to North America on the Reading Railroad in 1938. On the left is coach-observation No. 304, one of five cars built for the Reading *Crusader*. CN purchased this train set in November 1963 and pressed it into service on their Montréal–Québec City *Champlain*. Here, trailing the July 24, 1980, National Railroad Historical Society convention special, the 304 waits as northbound VIA train No. 3, the *Super Continental*, arrives alongside the station platform at Allandale, Ontario. Today, the 304 is preserved at the Railway Museum of Pennsylvania. *Robert Sandusky*

Unseasonably cold temperatures are evident as copious amounts of steam rise off the eastbound *Atlantic* during a stop for fuel and water at Brownville Junction, Maine, on New Year's Day 1981. The matched set of MLW cab units are running more than five hours late and have completed just half of their trek through Maine. *George Pitarys*

named trains: the *Bonaventure*, the *Cavalier*, and the *Lakeshore*. Each train provided the same standard of onboard customer service as the *Rapidos*, but stopped at a number of points along the line and thus took an extra hour to reach the terminus. Overnight service aboard the *Cavalier* gave travelers and businesspeople the opportunity to rest en route and to arrive refreshed and energized at their destination, in time for an early engagement.

Although CN continued to lose money overall, passenger revenues and ridership continued to climb. A concerted effort to upgrade fixed plant in the Corridor by replacing jointed rail with continuously welded rail helped to decrease the scheduled time between cities and increase passenger comfort through a better ride. By contrast, the CPR discontinued its sole remaining pair of Corridor trains between Montréal, Ottawa, and Toronto by the end of 1965. CN now had a monopoly over Corridor rail passenger service and anticipated a record level of service nationwide heading into Canada's centennial year of 1967.

Delagrave continued his push for more frequent and improved service, and although he would succeed, it would eventually cost him his job. Moreover, the federal political climate was finally stable enough to allow the recommendations of the MacPherson Report for subsidization of passenger rail service to be enacted into law under a new National Transportation Act, sowing the seeds for a singular body whose mandate would be to maintain a nationalized rail passenger network. Yet by the time Canada's Centennial had passed, the same seeds remained dormant and continued to hibernate for a decade longer. The inception of VIA Rail was still more than 10 years away.

CP Rail RDC-3 No. 9021 leads a sister RDC-2 through Bayview Junction on May 28, 1978, as part of the CP's Toronto–Hamilton–Buffalo "Dayliner" service. This route was still operated by CP until a subsidiary service request handed control over to VIA on March 30, 1979. *W. Townsend photo, author collection*

CHAPTER TWO

TOWARD NATIONALIZATION: *1967–1974*

In 1967, both Class 1 railways in Canada, and especially their passenger services, were on the brink of a financial calamity. Anticipated record levels of passengers traveled by rail throughout the nation for its centennial year but did not provide the windfall required to overcome passenger service losses. The railways had a problem on their hands and demanded relief from escalating expenses, federal mandates to maintain unprofitable passenger and freight routes, and the loss of lucrative railway post office services to air and road transportation agencies. Both CN and CPR were fearful of railway meltdown and looked to the government to resolve the issue through legislation.

It is undeniable that intercity rail passenger services in most regions of North America are at worst unprofitable and at best a break-even venture. The late Buck Crump defined the issue as "a function of population and distance: the higher the nation's density per square mile, the greater chance of railroading success." Perhaps the only successful application of this formula in postwar Canada is the densely populated region between Québec City, Québec, and Windsor, Ontario. The Corridor, as it is commonly known, has traditionally yielded the most revenue per passenger mile, while possessing the fewest number of train miles. The majority of train miles run outside this region, east to the Maritimes and west toward the Pacific Ocean, mostly due to the geographic makeup of Canada. As a result, eastern and western transcontinental services have normally generated the least amount of revenue per passenger mile and have incurred the highest deficits.

Until the mid-1960s, railways offset such losses through a form of internal cross-subsidization. The expense of passenger

The *Canadian* approaches the grain elevators of Indus, Alberta, under threatening skies on July 29, 1979. Safe from the storm, passengers enjoy a drink in the Mural Lounge of dome-observation No. 15411, *Revelstoke Park*. During the construction of the 18 *Park*-series cars, Canadian Pacific commissioned 18 Canadian painters to create murals depicting the namesake national park in each Mural Lounge. In 1986, the paintings were removed for restoration but were left out of the cars following the HEP refurbishment program, replaced by more modern works. *Richard Yaremko*

Routing for VIA's western transcontinentals changed several times between 1978 and 1990. Starting with the October 29, 1978, timetable, the *Canadian* operated from Toronto, while the *Super* originated in Montréal, changing the former method of two short trains meeting and combining in Sudbury and Capreol, respectively. During this iteration, the *Super* had an unusual routing over the CP's M&O Subdivision to Ottawa, which only lasted until June 1979, when the eastern terminus for both name trains was switched. In October of that year, the two trains combined at Sudbury to operate over CP tracks to Winnipeg, where they split and went their separate ways. This practice reverted back to two separate name trains in June 1981 until the *Super* was discontinued on November 15. Following the 1981 cuts, the *Canadian* was rescheduled along the Corridor from Montréal to Toronto and then north to Sudbury. The reintroduction of the *Super* on June 1, 1985, yielded a return to the traditional CP-style operation of the *Canadian*, while the *Super* remained a Winnipeg–Vancouver train until 1990. In this photo, the *Canadian* speeds north past the St. Clair Avenue station as it departs Toronto on CN's Newmarket Subdivision on May 8, 1979. Once past Washago it would switch over to the all-CPR route west. *Robert Sandusky*

Still wearing the red CN logo, VIA FP9 No. 6516 leads a GMD-MLW lash-up stopping at the Dufferin Street entrance to the Canadian National Exhibition fairgrounds on September 1, 1979. This platform was only opened for use during special events and saved a long trip back from Union Station for non-GO passengers. It has since been replaced by a GO Transit station. *Robert Sandusky*

operations were factored into a railway's cost base and paid for through increased freight rates—a kind of invisible "tax" for the maintenance of rail passenger service. As the 1960s progressed, however, competition for freight service between the railways and other modes of transport became increasingly fierce, and continuing losses incurred by passenger train service could not easily be covered by the existing cross-subsidization paradigm; passenger trains were becoming a burdensome issue for the railways.

In view of public demand for the maintenance of passenger services, neither CN nor CPR abandoned outright their support for passenger trains. In fact, CN maintained a firm and innovative commitment to passenger trains, viewing them as both beneficial and essential for Canada. Representing themselves before the House of Commons' Standing Committee on Transport in 1966, both railways offered their views and expectations concerning the "effective demand" of the traveling public and illustrated their commitment toward the provision of service. The approach of the privately owned CPR was unsurprisingly analogous to that of most roads in the United States, merely alluding to their belief in upholding a public service after having curtailed passenger train service in the wake of their revitalization attempts of the 1950s and abdicated the pooling arrangement within the Corridor. "Effective demand is the demand for a service at prices which meet the cost of providing that service . . . the policy of The Company has always been to meet fully the effective demand for passenger service and it intends to do so in the future. . . . The [CPR] has never [abandoned a service] until after its studies established that effective demand has gone and could not be recovered."

Quite the reverse, the testimony from representatives of Canadian National noted their railway's efforts throughout the early 1960s to revive the passenger train while seeking a balance between a public service and their bottom line. For the CN, "effective demand . . . [came] about only with an effective effort and effective service."

The 1967 National Transportation Act

By 1966, demand to remedy the situation of the railways had climaxed. Increasing pressure from both the CN and CPR to adopt a liberalized and open-market approach, combined with public opposition to potential passenger service discontinuation, compelled the government to act. The National Transportation Act (NTA) of 1967 was devised as a means of realigning federal policy to better address the needs and issues of a burgeoning and multifaceted transportation industry in an integrated and coherent manner while curtailing public spending and avoiding the wrath of public opinion in the face of potential service discontinuances. The conclusions of the MacPherson Commission on Transportation six years previous recognized the realities of the contemporary Canadian transportation industry and suggested that passenger services by the railways, except where essential or economically viable, were no longer required. Yet, amid nationalist sentiment during the yearlong centennial celebrations, the government understood that heeding the cold business logic of the MacPherson Commission would be political suicide. Citing the 100-year-old constitutional promise, public opinion demanded that rail services be maintained, rendering the subsidy of rail passenger services a political necessity.

The stance of the Canadian government toward rail passenger service became preservationist and completely ignored the findings of the commission. In the mind of the government, the passenger train problem was merely a "market failure in which the full value of the train's employment, access and mobility benefits were not recovered from the fares that were being paid." The path toward full passenger rail subsidization took a giant leap forward when Parliament and its agencies, through the NTA, attempted to overcome these deficiencies by arbitrating the restructuring of passenger services and offering to cover, at public expense, a limited portion of the losses incurred. At the same time the government encouraged the railways to cooperate by improving service, cutting costs, and eliminating duplicate services and routes.

The Canadian Transport Commission

Transport Minister Jack Pickersgill, who believed that passenger services were obsolete and retention meant keeping "a few trains, but only in a museum," also thought that the NTA would provide a means for the railways to eliminate all rail passenger services without public recourse. Regrettably for Pickersgill, the timing of the legislation could not have been more inopportune, with public interest in the railways and passenger services at their zenith. He would have to find another way to ensure the demise of the passenger train, and the legislation he introduced created a bureaucratic vehicle that might provide just such an opportunity. Pickersgill resigned from government on September 20, 1967, to become president of this new agency the very next day.

Through the merger of the Board of Railway Commissioners, the Air Transport Board, and the Canadian Maritime Commission, the NTA created the Canadian Transport Commission (CTC) to oversee the new subsidy arrangement. The NTA authorized the CTC (through its Rail Transport Committee) to reimburse each railway up to 80 percent of their deficit for uneconomic routes while the railroads themselves were to

6713
6713
6713

In accordance with a prohibition of diesel engines operating inside the Mount Royal Tunnel, CN Class Z-1a boxcab electric locomotives 6713 and 6714 lead VIA FP9 No. 6530 and train up the 5.7-kilometer underground grade where they will egress at the Canora portal (Portal Heights) and stop in front of the Mount Royal commuter station. Here, on June 29, 1984, they will uncouple from the passenger train and clear the main to allow the VIA train to continue north. *R. Palmer photo, author collection*

Once considered a prime route for LRC service, the short two-car consist of the Edmonton–Saskatoon local traverses the undulating prairie landscape near Ardrossan, Alberta, on April 1, 1983. The introduction of the Winnipeg–Saskatoon–Vancouver *Panorama* just over a year later replaced this local service. *Richard Yaremko*

bear the 20 percent balance as "an incentive to economic efficiency." Per the subsidy arrangement, the CTC held authority over the disposition of existing routes and permitted railways to "discontinue services no longer required . . . [end] unnecessary duplication and eliminate any over-capacity . . . on services that [were] required to continue operating in the public interest." The NTA thus relieved the railways of the financial burden of unprofitable passenger services, placing them on an equal footing with competing modes of transport without discharging them of their obligation to maintain passenger trains.

Irrespective of whether a railway wanted to discontinue a service or receive subsidy funding, it was required to apply for discontinuance. The application resulted in a CTC review that was open to public input to determine if said passenger train was truly uneconomic or the service should be continued under subsidy in the public interest.

The Politics of Discontinuance

After a series of minority governments throughout the 1960s, the Liberal Party with Pierre Trudeau at the helm attained a majority government in the 1968 election. For the first time in five years, the governing party was able to enjoy a certain level of political safety and freedom to pass legislation despite opposition. Following the election and the establishment of the CTC, a series of patronage appointments for services rendered to the Liberal Party stacked the ranks of the CTC with individuals politically sensitive to the government's agenda. More so than ever before, the whim of government politicized the survival or demise of rail passenger service and the direction and scope of subsidy dollars.

The first and most notable effort of either railway to cease passenger operations that provided insight into public reaction concerning discontinuance occurred in Newfoundland. CN applied to the CTC in 1967 to replace its provincial passenger services with "unquestionably clean, modern and fast buses." In spite of staunch opposition from a voting public that scorned the replacement of onboard dining car facilities and overnight sleeping car services with a 15-hour bus ride, the federal government, and the CTC under Jack Pickersgill, remained steadfast in their support and execution of the discontinuance application. The outcome was a public relations nightmare that resulted in the loss of six of seven provincial seats in the 1968 federal election.

The Newfoundland experience, combined with public outcry in the United States after the systemic purging of most U.S. rail passenger routes with the creation of Amtrak, had much to do with government adopting an increasingly protectionist attitude toward rail passenger service despite evidence showing a continual decline in passenger train miles between 1968 and 1975. At the same time, Prime Minister Trudeau had deeply committed government to the development of a domestic airline industry and investment in two airport megaprojects that yielded intense public protest and dissension.

Each discontinuance hearing the railways applied for from this point forward was well attended and sometimes dominated by vociferous proponents of service retention. Fear of additional discord contributed to the preservationist attitude the government adopted after 1970. Thus, the Trudeau government reined in the CTC, who permitted the abandonment of only 14 more services while ruling for the continuance and subsidization of some 59 routes. Although most services may indeed have been unprofitable, the CTC nevertheless concluded that none were in fact uneconomic and based their conclusions entirely on nonmarket criteria such as the future demand for and current or potential quality of services offered.

Carleton University professor Julius Lukasiewicz, one of the more learned critics of the NTA subsidy mechanism, had a clear understanding of interactions between government and the CTC. According to Lukasiewicz, federal government policies concerning rail passenger service were "limited to passive regulation and protection of past practices" and passenger rail abandonment and subsidy provisions of the 1967 NTA were used to

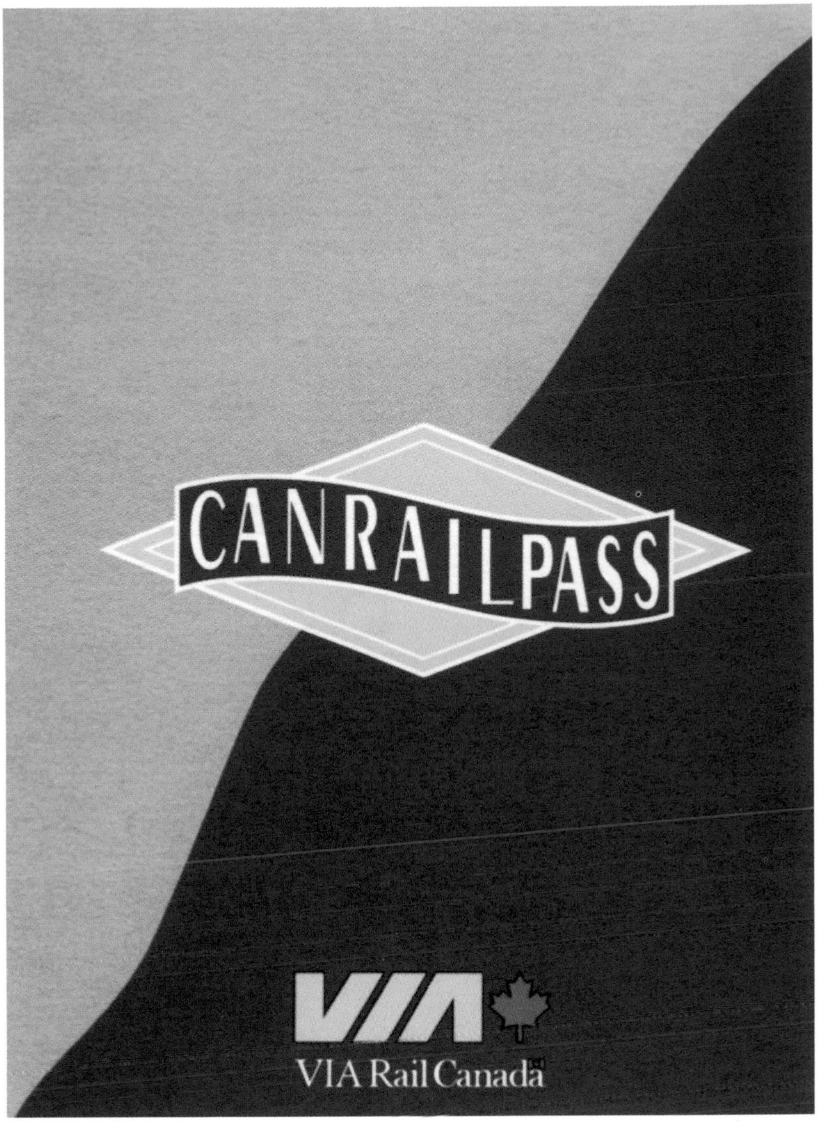

Anticipating a large volume of passenger traffic during the centennial year, CN first introduced the CANRAILPASS in 1964. Today, holders of a VIA CANRAILPASS can enjoy 12 days of unlimited economy-class travel during a 30-day period. ***Author collection***

maintain rather than discontinue passenger trains "at a high cost to the public." Ostensibly, this approach was an effective political tool to defer the problem until a later point in time in order to diminish the issue in the eye of the voting public. Unfortunately for the ruling Liberals, this tactic would not survive the 1970s and once more, the passenger train problem would be thrust to the forefront of public attention. The formation of a nationalized rail passenger service was almost inevitable.

Pressing Forward

Despite political debate and financial concerns, both railways pressed forward with their respective philosophies on rail passenger service throughout the early to mid-1970s. Although CN and CP (which altered their corporate image in 1968, changing their name to "CP Rail") flirted with and, in the case of the former, implemented high-speed trains in an attempt to compete with the airline industry, each railway's approach to the passenger train dilemma remained more or

Once a major division point for the CN, railway action in Capreol, Ontario, is much subdued compared to its heyday. Since 1990, the small hamlet hosts the *Canadian* six times per week. On March 6, 2003, the westbound consist has arrived on time at 3:58 p.m. to change crews and take on fuel. *Author collection*

VIA train 692, the *Hudson Bay*, takes the siding at Wabowden, Manitoba, to clear the main line for its northbound counterpart led by FP9ARM No. 6302 on September 20, 1995. Once clear, 692 will back out and approach the station before continuing south to Winnipeg. Northern Manitoba is also the last bastion of mixed-train service in Canada. While the Wabowden–Churchill mixed discontinued in 2002, VIA continues to operate a local mixed train between The Pas and Pukatawagan. *Ted Ellis*

less in line with their statements before the House of Commons' Standing Committee on Transport some 10 years previous.

However, discontented attitudes among upper management remained and the image presented to the public in favor of service retention masked a discontent with providing mandated-yet-unprofitable services, exacerbated by having to offset one-fifth of passenger train losses as per the 80 percent subsidy agreement. The elimination of all Railway Post Offices (RPOs) in 1972 incensed railway executives even further as it removed a key source of revenue. For many secondary passenger routes and branch-line freight services, RPOs were a saving grace whose loss was not recoverable by funding from the NTA subsidy agreement.

CN welcomed Norman MacMillan in 1967 as successor to Donald Gordon. MacMillan was fond enough of passenger trains and was personally indifferent to the technicalities of the 80 percent subsidy, content to adopt a laissez-faire attitude, claiming that if the CN was "going to run the passenger business, we might as well run it as best as we can." In the meantime, other CN executives, including Dr. Robert Bandeen, who was well versed and much involved in passenger operations since the days of Pierre Delagrave,

Good company, lively tunes, and a generous helping of spirits keep the party going inside the Bistro Car. Discontinued by CN in 1975, former patrons of this service fondly remember indulging themselves only to be "poured" out upon reaching their destination, just like the drinks they enjoyed. *CN photo, Coo/West collection*

thought differently of the issue and encouraged MacMillan to divest the railway of its unprofitable operations, at least as much as possible under the NTA.

Bandeen's efforts to improve the bottom line under the presidency of Norman MacMillan may have been more far-reaching were it not for government pressure placed on Jack Pickersgill and the CTC after 1970. The only major schedule change after the discontinuances in Newfoundland was the disappearance of the *Panorama* from the timetable in 1970. An attempt to terminate the *Super Continental* the following year was made to no avail as the CTC denied the application.

CN continued a much reduced, quasi-effort to attract passengers to its trains. Since the end of the pool train agreement in 1965, the CN held a near monopoly in the Québec City–Windsor Corridor and implemented several revitalization ideas designed to decrease costs to travelers. The sometimes

controversial and always mechanically troublesome *TurboTrain*, which was introduced in 1968 for high-speed service between Montréal, Toronto, and Ottawa, decreased travel time and was touted as a preferred choice for the business traveler. Those wishing to travel

Six months after VIA became a Crown corporation, the red and white livery of leased CN MRE-18g Nos. 3152 and 3154 belie the ownership of this train. Only the last three of the seven coaches in this *Tempo* consist have received VIA paint, but the train nevertheless looks striking amid the colorful October 1978 foliage. *Robert Sandusky*

at a more leisurely but festive pace could ride one of two Bistro cars featuring a pianist in vaudevillian apparel on the afternoon *Rapido* between Toronto and Montréal. For service within the Corridor west of Toronto, a fleet of 25 lightweight aluminum side cars known as *Tempo* trains were led by refurbished and brightly colored road switcher units in southwestern Ontario.

In 1972, only a year after it was prohibited from ending long-distance services west of Ontario, CN introduced two innovative

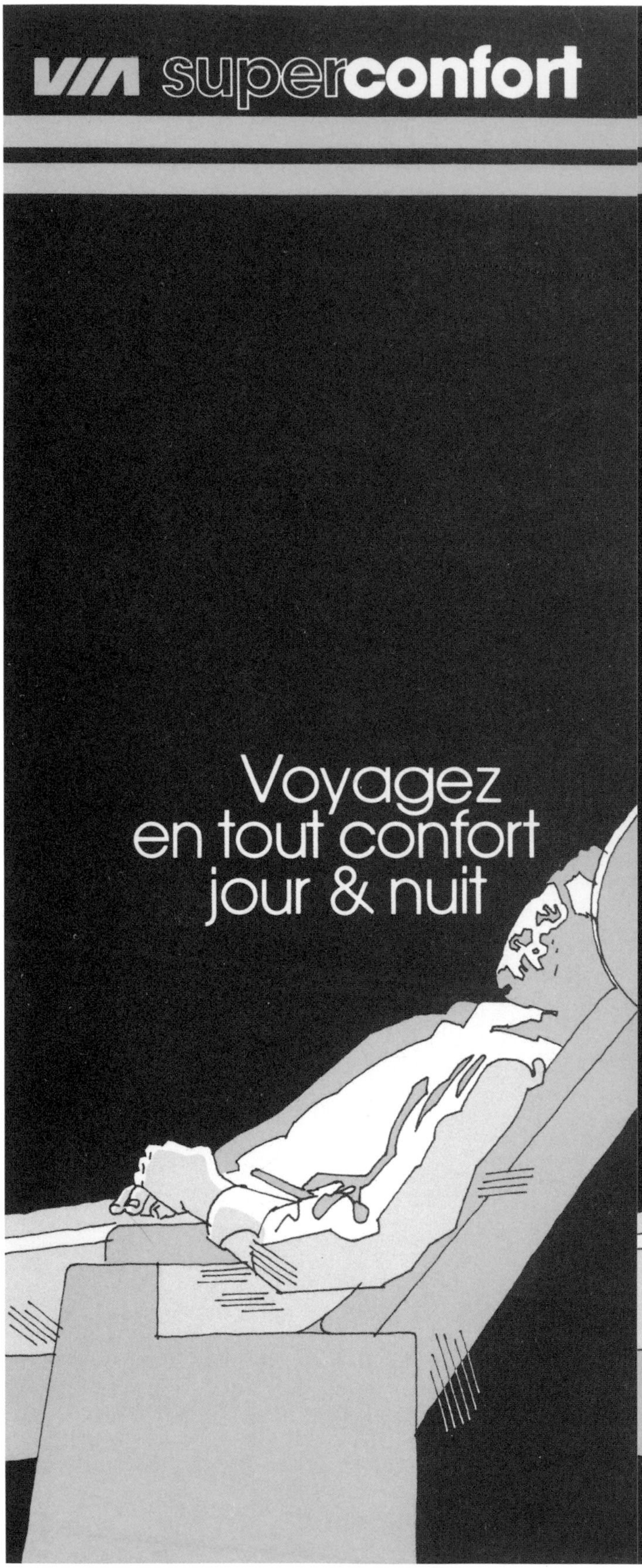
VIA superconfort
Voyagez
en tout confort
jour & nuit

VIA dayniter
for
comfortable
travel
night & day

One of eight automobile boxcars repainted for the Auto-With-You service offered between Toronto and Edmonton on the CN's *Super Continental*. VIA discontinued this amenity in June 1978. *CN photo, Canada Science and Technology Museum, CN Image Collection No. E2698-3*

concepts in transcontinental service. Devised as a more comfortable yet affordable accommodation either during daylight hours or overnight for the economically minded traveler, the *Dayniter* coach featured larger seats with extended leg rests that reclined farther than those aboard a regular coach. Auto-With-You was an expansion of CN's Car-Go-Rail program and offered transcontinental customers on the *Super Continental* between Toronto and Edmonton the option to ship their vehicles aboard the same train on which they traveled. Both ideas were successful with customers and buttressed their support for rail passenger service.

Attitudes toward passenger service at Canadian Pacific were far less ambiguous than at CN and the majority of CP's applications to the CTC for discontinuance were intended as a means of abolition. In addition to the preponderance of name trains already dropped from their schedule after 1967, the CPR made a marked but futile effort to dispose of its crack train, *The Canadian*, two years later. The CTC mandated the railway to maintain a seven-car minimum consist, essentially a skeleton version of what it once was. The CPR increasingly regarded its now "obligatory" service as inconsequential to its operation and adhered to only the statute's bare minimum. Moreover, significant fare increases aided in diverting ridership to either the CN or other modes of travel, thereby exacerbating CPR's losses on passenger service and fostering the claim that it was no longer sustainable.

Reductions in rail passenger service subsidies under the National Transportation Act

Opposite: A promotional brochure for VIA's *Dayniter* service, also called *Supercomfort* in French. As a Crown corporation, VIA has always published its material in both official languages of Canada. *Jason Shron collection*

A mishmash of CN and VIA colors appears on the diverse selection of coach and sleeping-car equipment on the *Super Continental* during the afternoon of July 5, 1978, near Jasper, Alberta. Note the Sceneramic dome 10 cars back from the locomotives. *John C. Benson*

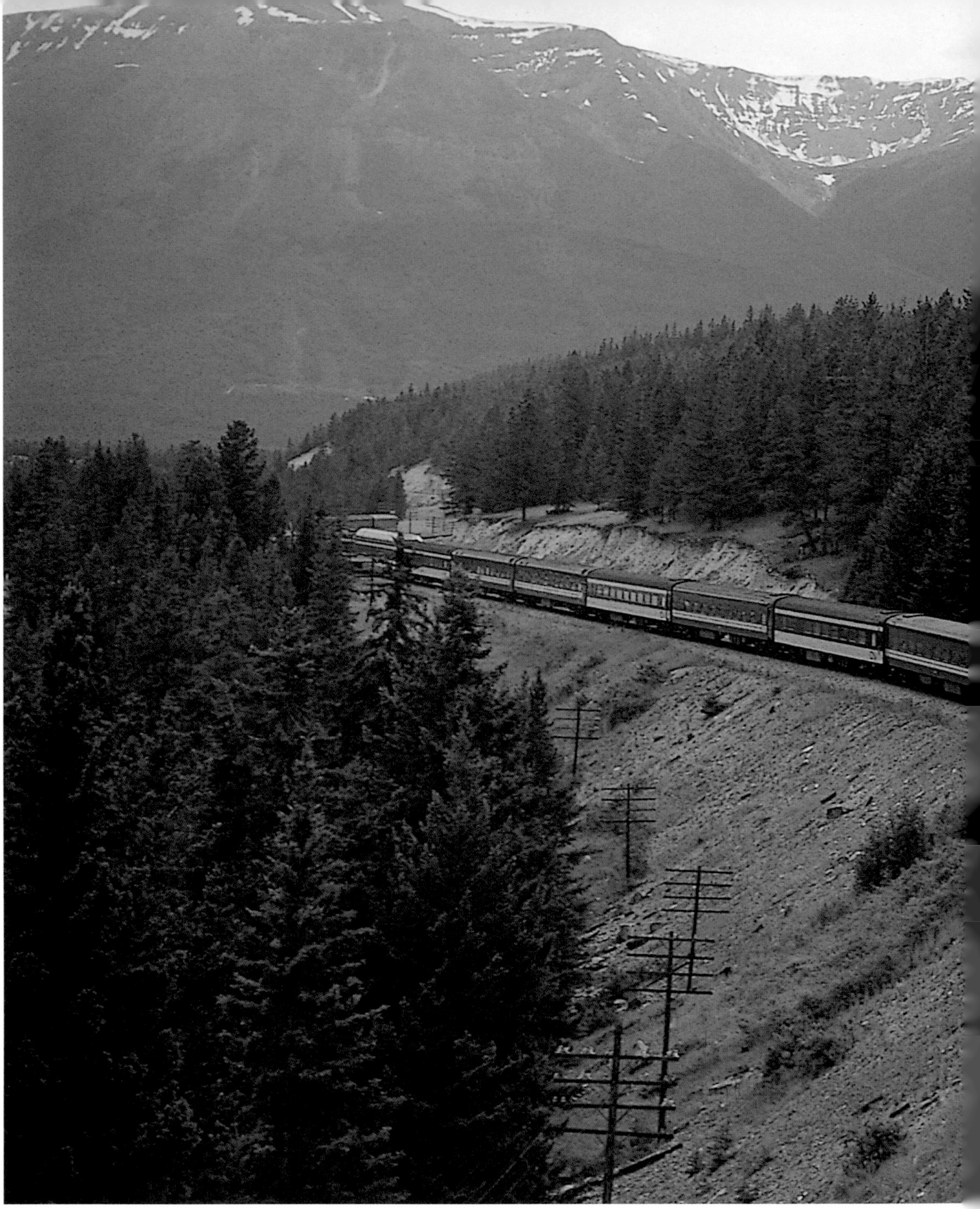

were intended to bottom out by 1974, but instead the amount increased threefold, by 1976 comprising 68 percent of all government funding to the railways. Little incentive existed for the railways to ameliorate the disposition of passenger services under the costing order of the subsidy arrangement, as they were prevented from receiving any additional funding for unprofitable passenger and freight routes until their claim for loss surpassed the amount of subsidy they were receiving. A variety of factors, including inflation, rising fuel costs, and internal efforts by the railways to discourage ridership led to cost overruns beyond existing subsidy levels far sooner than government had anticipated. Under these conditions, the cost to subsidize the network quickly spiraled out of control.

Regardless of efforts to remedy the passenger train problem, and despite federal

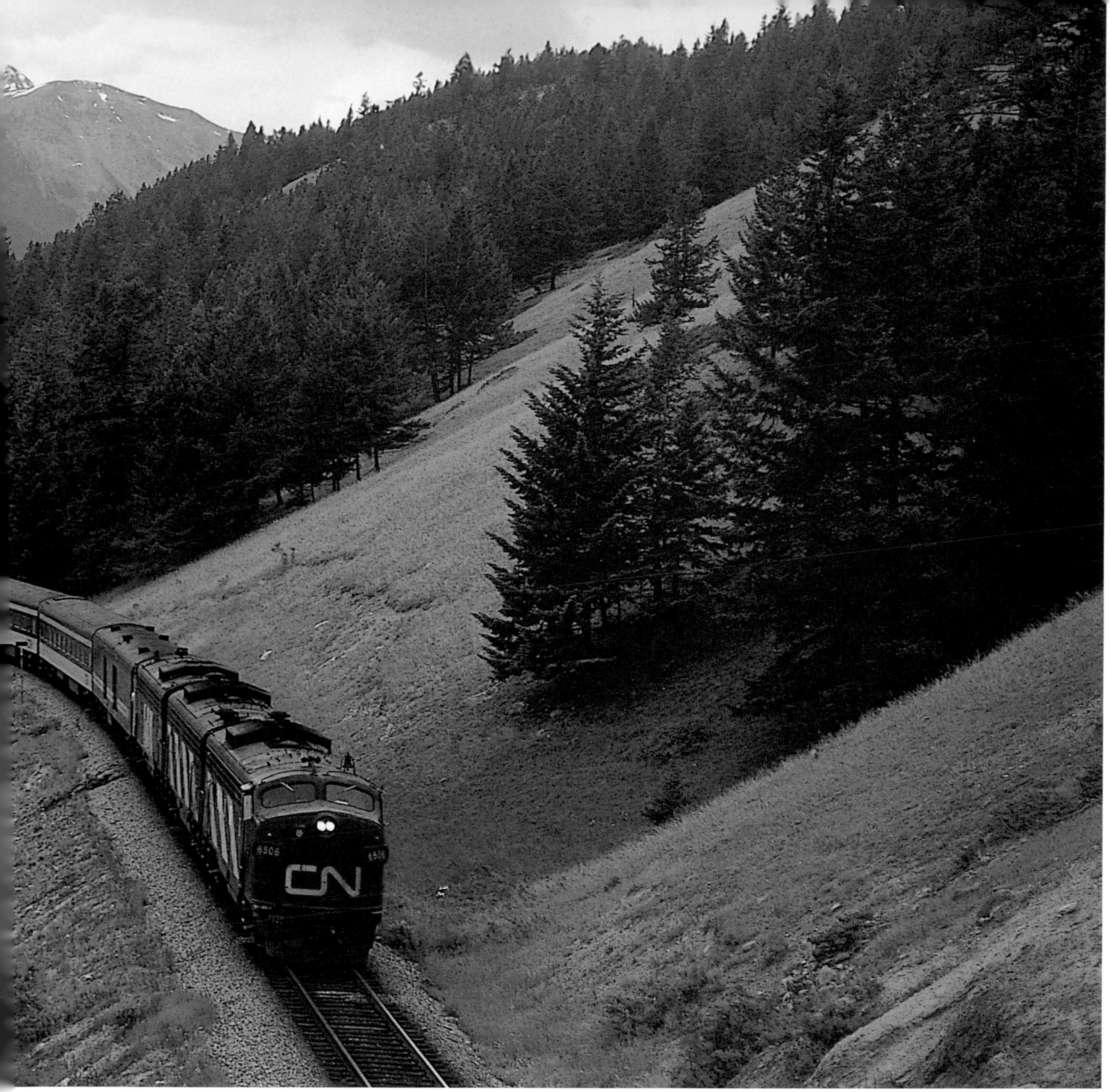

subsidy assistance, the CN was still losing several million dollars per year on passenger services. At CP, the financial situation for its emaciated passenger network was equally bleak. Government proponents of the 1967 NTA believed that "only some trains would become uneconomic" and the methodology of subsidization would ultimately alleviate the systemic losses in passenger service revenues. This prediction was sorely miscalculated and flew directly in the face of the MacPherson Commission, becoming a point of contention for the governing Liberal Party. Nevertheless, government remained uninterested in offsetting the remaining 20 percent of passenger service losses and maintained that the problem was a railway matter. Despite growing frustration toward overwhelming subsidy overruns, government remained loath to take decisive action.

At 3:55 p.m. in the afternoon of July 5, 1978, the eastbound *Super Continental* arrives in Jasper, Alberta, with both the east- and westbound versions of the Jasper–Prince George *Skeena* on the adjacent track. After the *Super* departs at 4:25 p.m., CN FP7Au 9174 will back her train out of the way, yielding to the westbound *Skeena* that departs at 4:45 p.m. the same day. *John C. Benson*

CHAPTER THREE

"We're Going All Out to Get You Where You're Going": *1974–1976*

Following the reelection of the Liberals with a strong majority government in 1974, winds of change swept through Transport Canada with the appointment of Jean Marchand as transport minister. Marchand took considerable interest in the issues that plagued the railways and as part of the Liberal's election mandate set about effecting change in government interaction with the railway industry.

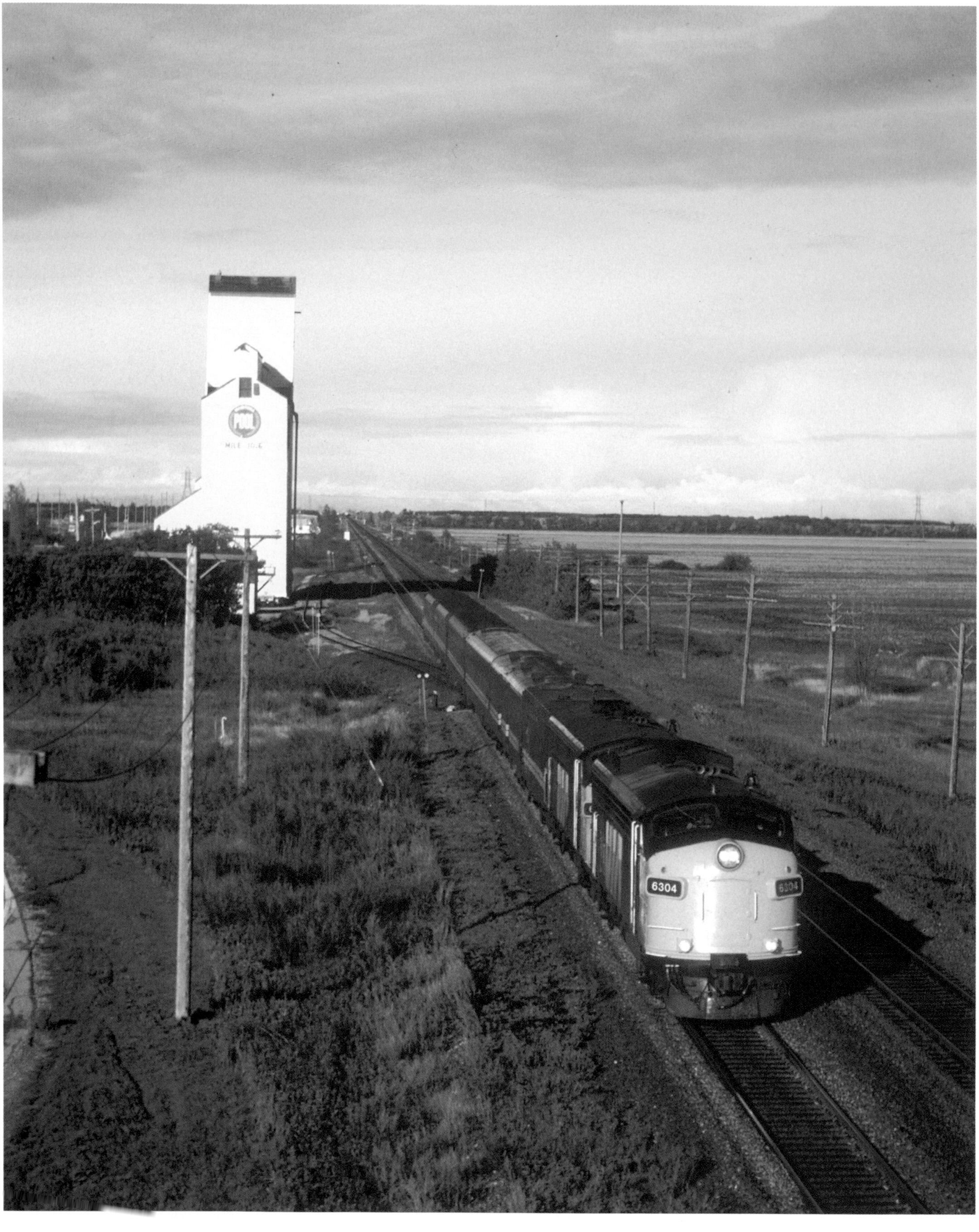

6304
6304

Marchand holistically viewed passenger transportation as an "instrument of national policy rather than as a passive support service" and as such, he outlined its priorities as being "accessible, equitable and efficient rather than economic, efficient and adequate."

Marchand also endeavored to stem the tide of resentment from the railways over their mandated losses under the 1967 National Transportation Act and believed that by encouraging a strategy of cost reduction, all those concerned would avoid the need for outright regulation. His position was supported by the recommendations of John R. Baldwin, former president of Air Canada *cum* consultant for the Ministry of Transport. In a report on transportation policy, Baldwin concluded that the rail passenger system was by and large mature with strong competitive elements. As such, "public interest in passenger transportation [was] best served by giving carriers increased commercial freedom while promoting stronger and fairer competition between carriers." Baldwin was concerned less with the developmental aspects of transportation and more with "rationalization" of the existing system over time, a concept that would dominate in the years to come.

Opposite: The sun has barely breached the horizon as VIA FP9ARM No. 6304 and the *Hudson Bay* pass the grain elevator at mile 10.6 of the CN's Rivers Subdivision and under the Perimeter Highway overpass, on time for a 7:30 a.m. arrival in Winnipeg on September 21, 1995. *Ted Ellis*

Plying the rails northward through the small town of Washago, Ontario, an A-B-A set of VIA Rail F units leads the *Super Continental* toward Sudbury and beyond on September 19, 1979. Just prior to arriving at their next stop of Parry Sound, FP9 No. 6541, F9B No. 6620, and FP9 No. 6523 will switch over to CP tracks at mile 146.1 (kilometer 235) of the CN's Bala Subdivision. The rounded windows on the sleeper behind the baggage car belie its heritage as one of five *River*-series sleeping cars so-named by the CN following their acquisition from The Milwaukee Road in 1966. Each car of this type remained in VIA service until 1990. *Author collection*

In anticipation of Thanksgiving weekend, FPA-4 No. 6773 is in charge of a nine-car holiday consist carrying travelers from Montréal to points west along the Corridor and Toronto on October 7, 1994. *Ronald J. Visockis, author collection*

In a speech to the House of Commons, Marchand suggested that CN and CP should collaborate in a manner similar to the former pooling arrangement, to become commercially viable by combining their passenger services and facilities wherever feasible to improve services with minimum cost.

Marchand also sought to redefine the role of the CTC with respect to the Ministry of Transport, believing that the purview of the CTC since its inception had far exceeded its original design. In order to affirm the chain of command for legislation and transportation policy in Canada, adjustments were necessary: "Transportation . . . is too big a business to dispense with an organization such as the CTC, but we would like to see the policy made by the Ministry of Transport and applied by the CTC. Right now, there are many fields where it is the CTC making the policy [and] not the department."

Unfortunately for Marchand, his view of the dilemma was outdated and did not reflect that of the railways, which increasingly viewed the subsidy arrangement as a liability and growing financial burden. For this reason alone, the CN and CP never bothered to initiate coordination and neither invested a large amount of new capital in passenger trains. By 1975, government regulation of passenger rail service was almost inevitable. Marchand never would have the opportunity to realize his ideas for railway reform as he was replaced by Otto Lang later the same year.

However brief, Marchand's stint as transport minister had a lasting impact on rail service in Canada. His vision of a regulated and nationalized network of rail passenger service formed, in part, the basis for the creation of VIA, though subsequent ministers of transport never acted on Marchand's interpretation of CTC authority to the extent that he envisioned, regardless of how effective it might have been in providing organizational clarity. Unfortunately, Marchand's comments on the interaction of the CTC and Transport Canada drew attention to the ambiguous division of jurisdiction, the immediate result of which was to pit two formidable bureaucratic entities against one another in a series of struggles over legislative authority that would affect the yet-to-be-created VIA Rail well into the next decade.

By Way of CN

In 1974, CN installed Dr. Robert Bandeen as president. Bandeen immediately tackled the subject of unprofitability on every segment of the Crown-owned railway. By 1975, CN reported a loss of several million dollars and Dr. Bandeen favored abolishing services over sustaining financial loss. His solution was the decentralization of operational sectors into a group of cost centers or subsidiary operating divisions as a means of trying to "get out from under the cost" of certain unprofitable services and shift the railway toward "profit-oriented autonomy." As such, the transfer of all CN passenger service assets to a separate rail passenger subsidiary marked the birth of VIA.

As an ancillary component of the larger railway, the new passenger subsidiary of CN remained obligated to operating passenger

A ticket sleeve from the author's first-ever trip on VIA with his parents by "technical proxy," and on the *Turbo* no less, between Kingston, Ontario, and Dorval, Québec—four months before his birth. ***Tom Greenlaw collection***

Standing on the vestibule stairs of the only sleeping car on train 58, a VIA/CN porter awaits passengers for the overnight run from Ottawa to Toronto. This E-series sleeping car was one of 52 built by Pullman for the CN in 1954, each named for Canadian cities beginning with the letter E and located along CN lines. *Canada Science and Technology Museum, CN Image Collection No. E3412*

services mandated by previous CTC rulings under the 80 percent costing arrangement. The advantage of separation from its parent company, on paper at least, was CN's ability to demonstrate to the nation both the potential and the financial shortcomings of a subsidized passenger concept. During an interview in May 2006, Bandeen revealed that CN opted in late 1975 to remodel their passenger subsidiary into a marketable, choice product for sale to consumers, taxpayers, and perhaps even the federal government, as CN had become fatigued with the perennial necessity of offsetting its 20 percent share of passenger losses and sought to obtain 100 percent compensation. Unless this were possible, the 1967 subsidy costing arrangement would continue into the next decade and CN would seek a means of completely divesting itself of the passenger train problem once and for all. Until then, they would give it one final push.

To promote their new passenger subsidiary, the CN harkened back to its successful reimaging campaign of the early 1960s and chose a color scheme, name, and logo for its passenger equipment. The creation of the name and logo fell on CN's Public Relations Department and their design examples were based on a livery of old gold and sapphire blue, personally selected by Dr. Bandeen in tribute to the colors of his former fraternity, Delta Upsilon. The PR department also selected the Latin word *via* as a title for the new subsidiary because it worked well in either of Canada's two official languages. When combined with the namesake of the railway, *via* provided the additional benefit of a marketing slogan that practically wrote itself. Its meaning was described to employees in one of the first VIA/CN newsletters as something that "dramatizes the commitment of [CN] to the rail passenger business and encompasses many improvements in passenger

amenities. VIA stands, quite simply, for the way to go: VIA CN." A stylized yellow logo, legible regardless of orientation, was created for the VIA name and was joined by a small, white Canadian National emblem in subscript to form "VIA [sub] CN." The combined image was placed at the end of a twin set of yellow stripes and applied over a blue background. With the addition of a marketing campaign led by the slogan, "We're going all out to get you where you're going," all that remained was to inaugurate the new service and cast out the VIA/CN lure to see if anyone was biting.

By Way of Otto Lang

Otto Emil Lang genuinely liked trains—that was a good thing for both the Trudeau government and for rail passenger service. In appointing Lang as transport minister in September 1975, the Trudeau Liberals would present and put into practice tangible solutions. For the time being, the passenger rail situation had a savior, and just in time.

Even though Marchand's plan for improving the issue of subsidies for passenger services contained viable and forward-thinking ideas that would be carried on under Lang's tenure, Marchand's agenda included support for the Baldwin Report's recommendation of "commercial self-sufficiency" best sustained through the substitution of "commercially viable bus services." Much to the chagrin of the highway bus industry, this would not come to pass with Lang at the helm.

Lang knew that rail passenger services were expensive to operate and even more so to subsidize. Government clearly did not

The long, enjoyable summer of 1987 is quickly drawing to a close as the October sun sinks below the horizon near Cobden, Ontario, enveloping the Sudbury–Montréal segment of the *Canadian* in a warm, red glow. FP9 No. 6507 and her five-car consist will continue into the night and arrive in Montréal around 10:30 a.m. *Andreas Kellar*

6771
VIA
6771

wish to keep decanting public funds in order to preserve a status quo that was not working. According to Lang, the general consensus among transport officials and the railways was that some nationalization of existing routes and markets was necessary if passenger trains were to continue in any form whatsoever. Moreover, the easiest way to manage a smaller, nationalized system of passenger services was through a single entity. What was once viewed solely as a railway problem had become a matter of national policy; Canada would at last join the list of major industrialized nations to view rail passenger services as a responsibility of the federal government.

The full support of government in combination with operational autonomy provides a level of freedom to effect change that is relished by those fortunate enough to enjoy it. Lang was granted such power by the Trudeau Liberals and, as a result, was able to genuinely think outside the box to lead the development of a manageable rail transportation system under the responsibility of the federal government. Soon after taking charge of the Ministry of Transport, Lang met with officials at CN where he learned more about their newly established passenger operating division. Lang was pleased with the VIA/CN concept, which was already established as a subsidiary and was administratively distanced from CN proper, creating the potential for its incorporation as a separate company. If regulation of all national passenger services was to occur, perhaps this was the vehicle Lang was looking for.

The creation of VIA/CN and government desire to formulate a plan for nationalized rail passenger service were concurrent but independently conceived. Based on the personal accounts of Bandeen and Lang, the government contacted CN very shortly after the VIA/CN program was publicized and, as a result, the marriage of the two ideas could not have been more opportune. To Lang, VIA/CN was the perfect tool for government to achieve its goal of regulated nationalization

Having left Sudbury around midnight, the *Canadian* rolls quietly across eastern portion of the Canadian Shield and into the scenic Ottawa River Valley, and will reach the national capital region before breakfast. By mid-morning, less than 40 miles (64 kilometers) remain of the more-than-2,880-mile (4,635-kilometer) transcontinental journey as the train skirts along the Lake of Two Mountains shoreline near Hudson, Québec. VIA FPA-4 No. 6771 leads the *Canadian* at the posted track speed of 55 miles (89 kilometers) per hour along CP's M&O Subdivision for an on-time arrival in Montréal at 11 o'clock. *Ted Wickson*

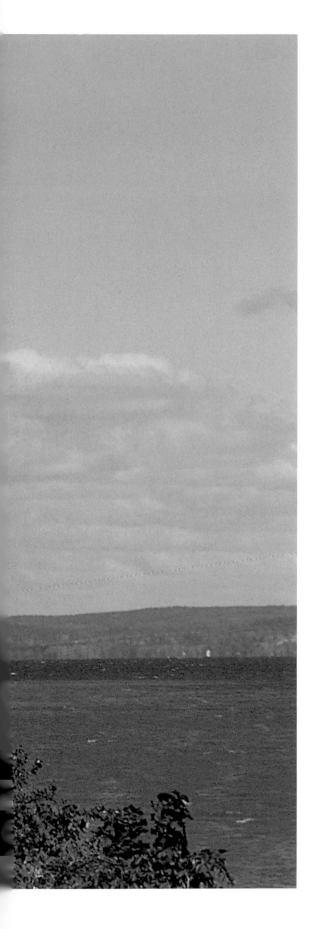

As FPA-4 No. 6793 with matched FPB-4s 6870 and 6871 quench their thirst for fuel and water during the dinner hour in Moncton, New Brunswick, on August, 3, 1983, VIA train 15, the *Ocean*, takes on passengers heading on to Miramichi, Bathurst, Campbellton, and other points west. *Alan Tillotson photo, author collection*

and maximize the rationalization of domestic passenger services. Bandeen was initially "shocked" by the expeditiousness of the government's move to capitalize on VIA/CN, but was content with the idea for economic reasons. Although the subsidiary company was still in development, CN was "delighted to get rid of it" so that they might focus on their more profitable freight services.

Before the House of Commons on January 29, 1976, Lang announced plans for "a basic network of inter city, coast to coast and commuter services [in coordination] with air and bus services" based on the paradigm of the MacPherson Commission. A document tabled by Lang the same day titled "Directive for the Guidance of the Canadian Transport Commission on Rail Passenger Services" provided amplifying instructions for the CTC to hold public hearings on the matter and develop plans to rationalize existing rail passenger services through subsidy reduction, elimination of duplicate services and some 2,000 route miles (3,219 kilometers), and operational and logistical consolidation. Naturally, the CP joined the negotiation procedures that had begun in earnest soon after the January announcement to Parliament. To the displeasure of rail subsidy opponents and supporters alike, the talks that would eventually determine the salient attributes of VIA took place behind closed doors.

Pros and Cons

In view of public demand for continuation of rail passenger service, both railways released statements that supported Lang's plan wholeheartedly, especially concerning elimination of some services to give priority to their freight services and respective bottom lines. At the negotiating table, however, the railways and government were at loggerheads over the way the new service would take shape. The CN and CP were of the same opinion that the government should pay the railways in full for all of their unprofitable services but disagreed as to the reorganization process of VIA. Although government initially proposed VIA to be a "unified CN subsidiary," CN wanted the entire VIA/CN wiped off its books and shunted off on its own as a Crown Corporation. For the CP, only the latter of the two choices was acceptable and they refused to approve an operation that would give its primary competitor access to proprietary information. Fortunately for CP, keeping VIA as a CN subsidiary would violate the legislation that governed their Crown-owned competitor and Lang was forced to examine other possibilities, delaying the incorporation of VIA as its own company until the following year. Meanwhile, despite the wrangling over its eventual operational form, the VIA/CN concept continued as planned in preparation for its official debut on March 25, 1976.

Criticism of VIA/CN abounded shortly after the official announcement of the subsidiary thrust the idea of a nationalized passenger railway into the public forum, but Lang was determined to "bull ahead" and overcome protest. In the midst of deliberations on a

On one of her last revenue service runs, this VIA *Turbo* travels along Montréal's West Island suburbs on July 3, 1982. A specially constructed servicing facility underneath Central Station in downtown Montréal would house at least two *Turbo*s for almost two years following their retirement on October 31, 1982. Unfortunately, all were scrapped. *Gordon E. Lloyd photo, author collection*

The cover of a CN condensed timetable issued for 1967, the year of Canada's centennial and the World Exposition in Montréal. *Author collection*

rationalized rail passenger network, the CTC commissioned a paper from the Institute for Guided Ground Transport on the pricing and subsidy of air and rail passenger transportation. Although the report concurred that the level of rail subsidies was both uncontrolled and generally ineffective, it argued that "conversion from an 80% to a 100% subsidy will only exacerbate [the problem]," and favored the benefits of other forms of transportation, arguing that "in contrast, the air subsidy program, while growing, appears to be [more] effective with regards to patronage and quality of service." Both the airlines and the highway bus industry took notice but bided their time on commenting.

Former Transport Minister and CTC President Jack Pickersgill was horrified by the government decision to involve itself in VIA and believed that the entire rail passenger system should be dismantled. Distaste for the Lang proposal for a nationalized passenger service was shared by Buck Crump. Pointing to CP's unsuccessful attempt to revitalize its passenger business in the late 1950s, Crump scoffed at the VIA/CN concept and stated that "there isn't a damn thing new about what Lang talked about and it won't work . . . because Canada's obsession with rail passenger service continues to ignore basic economic truths of the transportation business." Crump believed that potential for economically viable passenger rail services existed only in the Québec City–Windsor Corridor.

The year 1976 also saw the formation of a public interest group that was almost entirely pro-passenger rail. Transport 2000 Canada, a nonprofit organization, came together as the result of a new direction in federal passenger policy and would act as a voice of support, clarity, and reason throughout the creation of VIA as a Crown Corporation and into the next millennium.

Flirting with High-Speed Rail

During the creation of VIA/CN, high-speed passenger rail was often suggested as a possible means of competing with airlines and intercity buses. High-speed rail was a key component of the negotiations that led to VIA, and Otto Lang formally announced the government's intention to equip VIA with efficient high-speed trains. The available technology CN had already implemented and an ongoing research and development program that CP supported would be carefully examined to find the best high-speed equipment for VIA.

Attempts to speed up passenger train services date back to the mid-1960s when Pierre Delagrave managed the passenger operations department for the CN under then-President Donald Gordon. The large-scale application of faster passenger trains in the Corridor as a means of improving ridership and revenues can be traced directly to the innovations in passenger service that Delagrave brought to fruition, starting with the introduction of *Rapido* trains in 1963. Although *Rapido* services met their stated goals, Delagrave believed that an even faster schedule was necessary. Upon learning about a low-slung, aluminum-framed, gas turbine–powered train under development by the United Aircraft Corporation, Delagrave was captivated by its potential to triple revenues between Montréal and Toronto. He succeeded in persuading both Donald Gordon and Norman MacMillan (Gordon's eventual successor) to

Continuing its evaluation in southern Ontario between Toronto and Sarnia, prototype LRC locomotive JV1 and coach JV2 lead three *Tempo* cars as CN Extra 71 near Woodstock on November 13, 1975. *Coo/West collection*

The arrival of LRC units in 1981 provided VIA with an alternative to leasing MRE-18 road units from the CN to provide Head End Power (HEP) to their *Tempo* fleet. *Coo/West collection*

support bringing this new design, called *TurboTrain,* to the CN before 1967, just in time for Canada's Centennial and the World Exposition to be held in Montréal the same year. Other CN vice presidents did not share the passion that Delagrave brought to the *Turbo* project, and the initiative suffered from administrative discord and subsequent delay. Delagrave resigned in protest in December 1965, citing fellow executives' lip service to his fervent belief that *Turbo* would ultimately succeed in the revitalization of rail passenger services. *Turbo* would eventually make it onto the rails of the CN, though not for another three years; too late for the Expo and the Centennial.

Five seven-car *TurboTrain* sets were built by the Montreal Locomotive Works (MLW) under contract to United Aircraft Corporation of Canada and leased to CN. Finally introduced on December 12, 1968, the inaugural run was an embarrassing failure. Its passenger complement loaded with media personnel, the westbound *Turbo* had an argument with a meat truck over the contested space of a level crossing near Kingston, Ontario, and the collision was caught on film by a photographer from the *London Free Press* riding in the rear dome car. As though this public relations nightmare was not disastrous enough, *Turbo* was incessantly fraught with breakdowns and mechanical problems during its initial years of operation and the entire fleet was removed for repairs and modifications four times. Each lengthy service interruption was well publicized, adding to the storm of controversy over CN's expenditure of public money on such a seemingly problematic endeavor. By 1974, however, *Turbo* was back in the Corridor and, with the exception of one train set rendered unserviceable following a fire, its operational performance and reliability was much improved and more or less remained so until its retirement in 1982.

MLW was also involved in the development and construction of a second high-speed rail product in conjunction with Alcan Canada Limited and Dominion Foundries and Steel. The makers of the LRC (Light, Rapid, Comfortable) sought to avoid the poor performance standards and low serviceability experienced by *TurboTrain* during its first years of operation, the result of untested technology rushed from drawing board to implementation. A more conventional approach to production and motive power was adopted for the prototype LRC, which consisted of a single locomotive and coach, and was powered with a diesel electric prime mover rather than gas turbine engines. Construction of the LRC prototype was completed in 1973 and, like its high-speed cousin, included a lightweight welded-aluminum frame and a power-tilt banking system that allowed for increased speeds through corners on existing track.

Tests began in September of the following year on the CN main line near Montréal and, shortly thereafter, at the U.S. Department of Transportation test facility in Pueblo, Colorado. The performance of the LRC throughout its 7,000-mile (11,265-kilometer) roundtrip exceeded expectations and the prototype set a track record on November 11, 1974, traveling 1,096 miles (1,764 kilometers) in 11 hours and 10 minutes at an average speed of 98.6 miles (159 kilometers) per hour. The return leg also included a tour through the U.S. Midwest and a brief run on the corridor between Calgary and Edmonton, Alberta. Amidst corporate takeover negotiations between MLW and suitor J. Armand Bombardier Limited, domestic trials commenced in February 1975 between Toronto and Sarnia, Ontario, to determine interoperability of the LRC with the CN's *Tempo* fleet. Bombardier would finalize its acquisition of MLW two months later and the LRC program continued under Bombardier's insignia through its eventual delivery to VIA in 1981.

Bordered on one side by the mighty Lake Superior and on the other by slide detectors, train No. 2, the *Canadian*, passes through Mink Tunnel at mile 72.8 (kilometer 117) of the CP's Heron Bay Subdivision. *W. H. Coo, Coo/West collection*

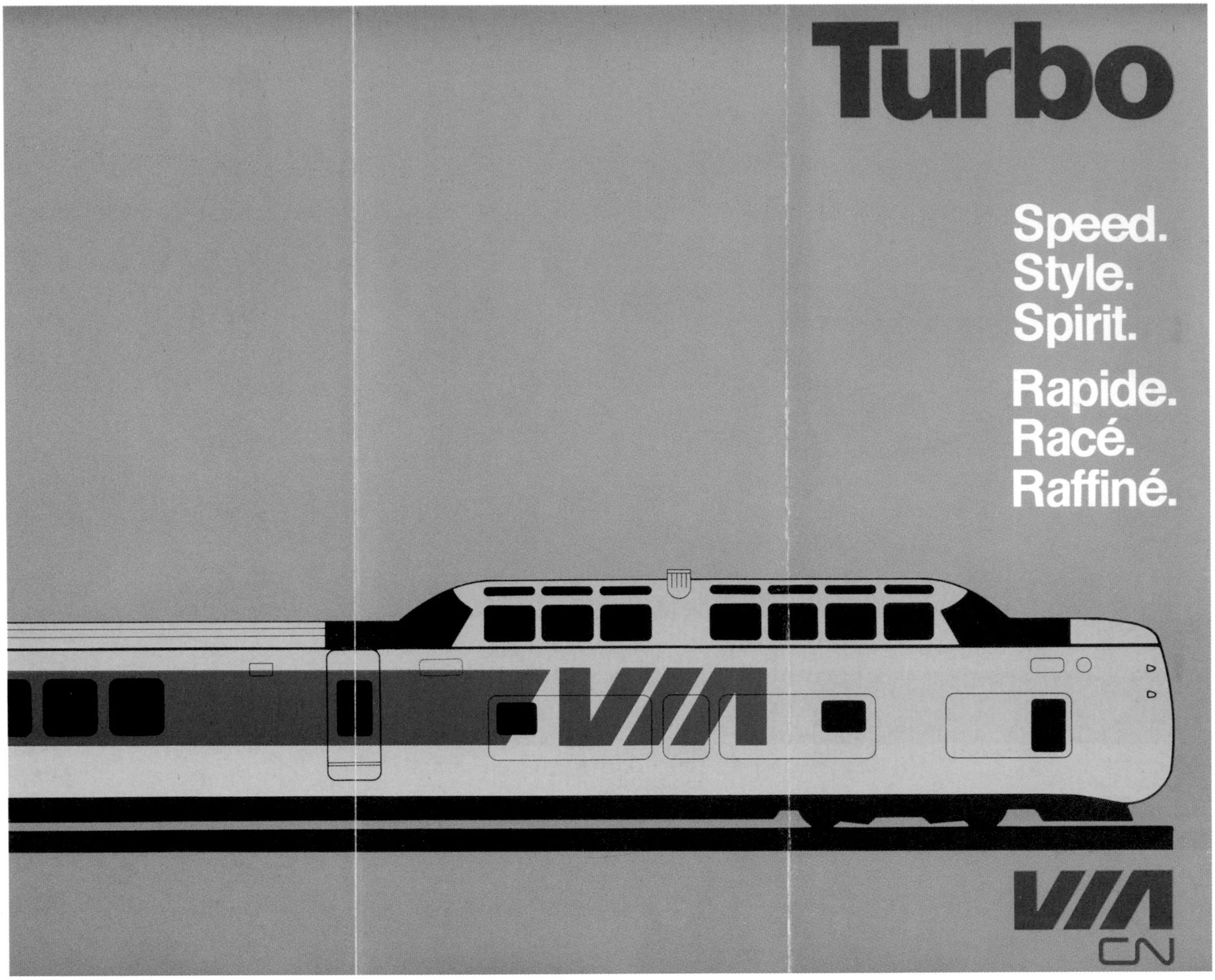

A 1976 VIA/CN brochure promotes *TurboTrain* services and amenities. *Jason Shron collection*

Thus, our story returns to the 1976 announcement of Otto Lang's intention to furnish VIA with high-speed trains. Debate on which program the government would champion dominated the negotiations with regard to VIA's routing and equipment considerations. Realistically, both projects were nothing more than an insincere flirtation by the government and the railways with the medium of high-speed rail because the majority of trackage along the *Turbo*'s route between Montréal and Toronto was jointed, contained sharp curves, and was fraught with level crossings, all nonconducive to high-speed operations. Although the technology utilized on the *Turbo* and LRC was designed to overcome some of these issues, specifically curvature and ride, the railways lacked the significant financial support and commitment from all levels of government to effect the changes necessary for a bona fide high-speed service, including the removal of all level crossings, straightening of the right-of-way, proprietary trackage for passenger services, and perhaps even electrification.

To its merit, *TurboTrain* had indeed overcome the numerous mechanical and operational hurdles from which it suffered and was finally coming into its own. Even so, the LRC program was favored as the program of choice for VIA based on its strong ties to the national research and development industry, an unfortunate development for CN and, by proxy, for taxpayers. Together they had invested a vast sum toward the development of the *TurboTrain* as a viable rail solution for Canadian travelers. For that reason, CN would not let their high-speed protégé roll out of the Corridor and into obscurity, and being the dominant factor in the VIA/CN gambit, CN would showcase the *TurboTrain* in a manner appropriate for a flagship train.

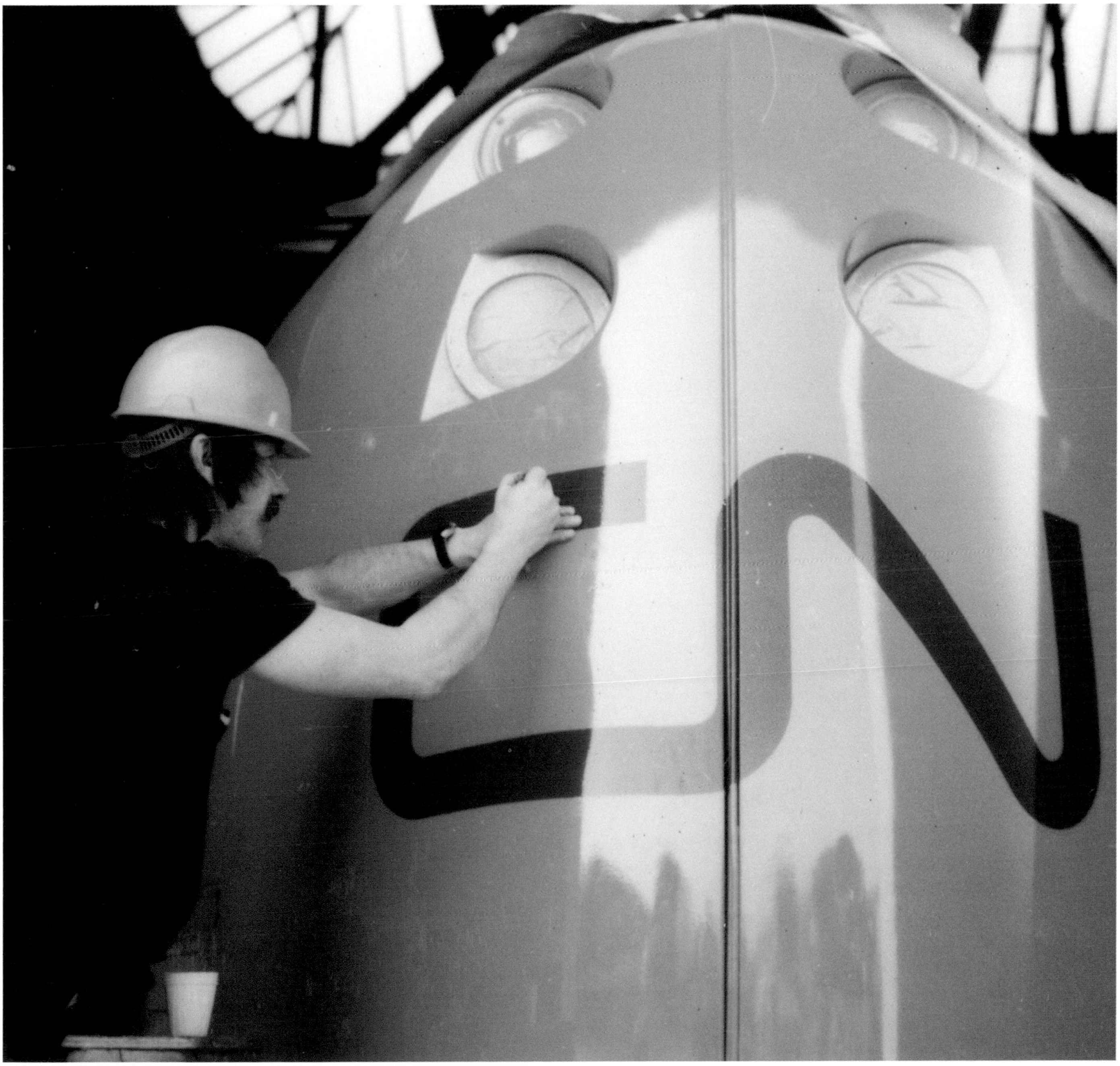

In preparation for the launch of the VIA/CN subsidiary, maintenance staff at the CN's Spadina roundhouse paint the *TurboTrain* in its new livery. The *Turbo* was the only VIA equipment to receive a yellow-dominant color scheme; the primary color for the rest of the fleet was blue. *Canada Science and Technology Museum, CN Image Collection No. E3323-16*

The *Turbo* breaks the land-speed record! CN camera and equipment operators record the historic event as the *Turbo* reaches a speed of 140.6 miles (226 kilometers) per hour. *Canada Science and Technology Museum, CN Image Collection No. 76069-15*

CHAPTER FOUR

TRANSITIONS: *1976–1980*

During the spring of 1976, Canadian railfans bore witness to two successful land-speed record attempts. The long-standing record of 115.5 miles (186 kilometers) per hour set on September 18, 1937, by Canadian Pacific F2a 4-4-4 Jubilee-class steam locomotive No. 3003 near mile point 38 of the Winchester Subdivision stood unchallenged in the Dominion for almost 39 years, until March 10, 1976, when

A classic A-B-A lash-up of cab units idles outside CN's Transcona shops in Winnipeg, awaiting their next assignment on April 20, 1978. The livery of lead unit No. 6504 is an example of the original VIA/CN paint scheme applied to VIA's F unit fleet in 1976. *Michael P. McIlwaine photo, author collection*

the LRC prototype reached 129 miles (208 kilometers) per hour during a test run south of Montréal. The excitement was far from over, however—the *Turbo* would have the last word.

While the official announcement of the new VIA/CN corporate image was set for April, 25, 1976, an eastbound *TurboTrain*, freshly painted in a striking new yellow and blue livery, quietly rolled out from beneath the train shed of Toronto's Union Station three days prior, carrying a complement of media and invited guests to "focus attention on the potential of passenger trains." Like CN's 1968 introduction of the *Turbo* on a similar public relations assignment, the media and passengers on the 1976 *TurboTrain* would also be treated to a historic event; however, this time it would be a triumph for the railway.

Shortly after Passenger Extra 153 departed Toronto, CN President Dr. Robert Bandeen along with Garth Campbell, now vice president of passenger marketing, held an onboard press conference regarding the new VIA/CN subsidiary and the anticipated changes for rail passenger service in Canada. All were treated to a meal before the train stopped in Kingston, where a final inspection was conducted. Safety preparations for the speed-record attempt along a 20-mile (32-kilometer) segment of continuously welded rail on the Kingston Subdivision were well underway: all switches were spiked and a CN employee personally guarded each level crossing. CN personnel also installed recording devices on the track and stood alongside a film and camera crew to record the *Turbo* as it made this historic attempt.

This eight-car train set was often seen in early VIA promotional material and made to look as though it was traveling through the Rocky Mountains. In reality, the consist was photographed near St-Bruno, Québec, and the mountainous background was superimposed. *Canada Science and Technology Museum, CN Image Collection No. E3499-17*

Adding to the excitement of what was about to occur, guests played a sort of musical chairs to find the best possible vantage point while ensuring they were still able to see the onboard closed-circuit television that broadcast a constant image of the train's speedometer. Clearing the yard limit at Brockville, the *Turbo* resumed its cruising speed of 95 miles (153 kilometers) per hour and shortly thereafter passed the approaches to the welded-rail section at mile 104 of the Kingston Subdivision where engineer John Shipman threw open the throttle. All eyes were glued to the speedometer reading on the televisions as the nine-car *TurboTrain* consist easily accelerated through the six-week-old record set by the LRC prototype. Guests were enthralled when at 3:55 p.m. on April 22, 1976, near Morrisburg, Ontario, the speedometer display read a staggering 140.6 miles (226 kilometers) per hour. Shortly after reaching its record speed, Norman de Poe, aboard this historic *Turbo* run for one of his last assignments as a journalist for the Canadian Broadcasting Corporation, remarked, "If God had intended man to fly, he wouldn't have given us the railroad." Without a doubt, the introduction of VIA was a success.

Following the record-breaking *Turbo* run, CN put its best foot forward to ensure that the government would make good on its 1976 announcement of intent to purchase the VIA/CN subsidiary. At a news conference in Toronto, Garth Campbell assured the public that rumors citing the end of passenger service in Canada were "greatly exaggerated." With the positive marketing of its subsidiary,

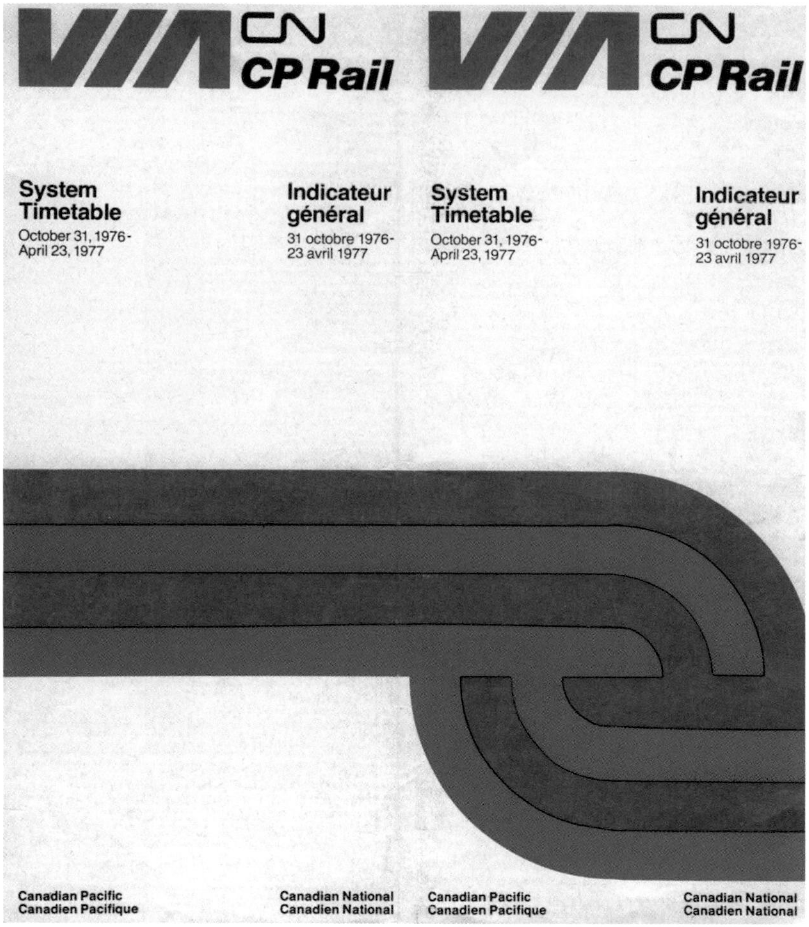

The October 31, 1976, timetable was the first to include scheduling information on both VIA/CN and CP Rail passenger services. ***Author collection***

bolstered by a change in scheduling, CN echoed governmental commitment to VIA/CN. One of VIA/CN's first ads summed up their approach to passenger services for the remainder of the year: "More trains where trains make sense, more service where it makes sense and fair fares everywhere; because at CN, the passenger business is alive and well."

Furthering the Cause

Although continuing negotiations on the final direction of the VIA/CN subsidiary would not gel until early 1977, the CN chose not to stand idly by during this long transition process. Rolling stock was painted in the new blue and yellow livery as it rotated through general maintenance cycles. Some cars were selected for refurbishment and would be part of an eight-car promotional train that toured the country to showcase the new image. CP's Stephen Morris amusingly refuted CN President Robert Bandeen's remark that the equipment of both railways would wear the blue and yellow color scheme once consolidated into a single fleet. In an interview with the *Ottawa Citizen*, Morris lamented that Bandeen jumped the gun because "blue and yellow would look 'hellish' on CP Rail's sleek stainless steel trains." Undaunted, VIA/CN also published its first

Just a few miles into its journey to the Pacific coast, VIA train No. 1, the *Canadian* will make its second stop on the Island of Montréal at the suburb of Dorval to entrain passengers before continuing west to Ottawa over the CP's M&O Subdivision. *Gordon E. Lloyd photo, author collection*

timetable with the image of a *TurboTrain* in the new livery proudly displayed on the cover.

Back in Ottawa, Transport Minister Otto Lang and his subordinates, along with the CTC, were hard at work through the waning months of 1976 on a series of formal proposals based on developments within the nationalization program thus far. The first of these concerned CN's railway passenger corporation, which had become an official subsidiary of the CN 12 days earlier under the title VIA Rail. This proposal recommended that the continuing effort to develop VIA should not result in discharging CN or CP of their "statutory obligation to run passenger trains" and that VIA should remain "responsible to government with regards to the provision of rail passenger service."

A second proposal released 48 hours later argued for the need to give VIA the legal status of a Class 1 rail operator in accordance with Section 11 of the Railway Act, one of

Once the eastbound consist of the *Canadian* is backed alongside the platform at VIA's Vancouver station, train staff make final preparations for an August 1990 departure. In order to assist passengers in finding their accommodations, the conductor arranges the line numbers to denote the order of each car on the train. *Coo/West collection*

the earliest documents to urge the formation of this new railway into its own Crown Corporation. With the exception of the latter, the most cogent elements of these proposals were acted upon and legislated with the insertion of a clause into the 1977 federal budget that appropriated only a single Canadian dollar. This clause, recorded as Transport Vote 52nd, was approved in Parliament without debate on March 29, 1977, and by government's own reckoning, was a means of "backdoor entry into public enterprise" that avoided the necessity for the "introduction into Parliament of a constituent Act for VIA." This legislative technique, while expeditious for policymakers, had a lasting negative effect on VIA by establishing it as a Class 1 railway without full articulation of its role and structure. Lacking an act of government pertaining directly to VIA, the new organization had no real mandate *per se* and as a result was further exposed than CN ever was to the politicized environment inherent in government and worse, to the whims of the ruling party.

Inheritance

Until this point, VIA Rail's organizational chart consisted of a notional chairman, a president, and some allocated office space. This began to change in March 1977 when VIA began hiring and transferring necessary personnel from CN's former passenger department to its yet unpopulated management and administrative departments. Concurrent with his presidency of the Canadian National, Bandeen had already assumed the role of VIA's first chairman and subsequently

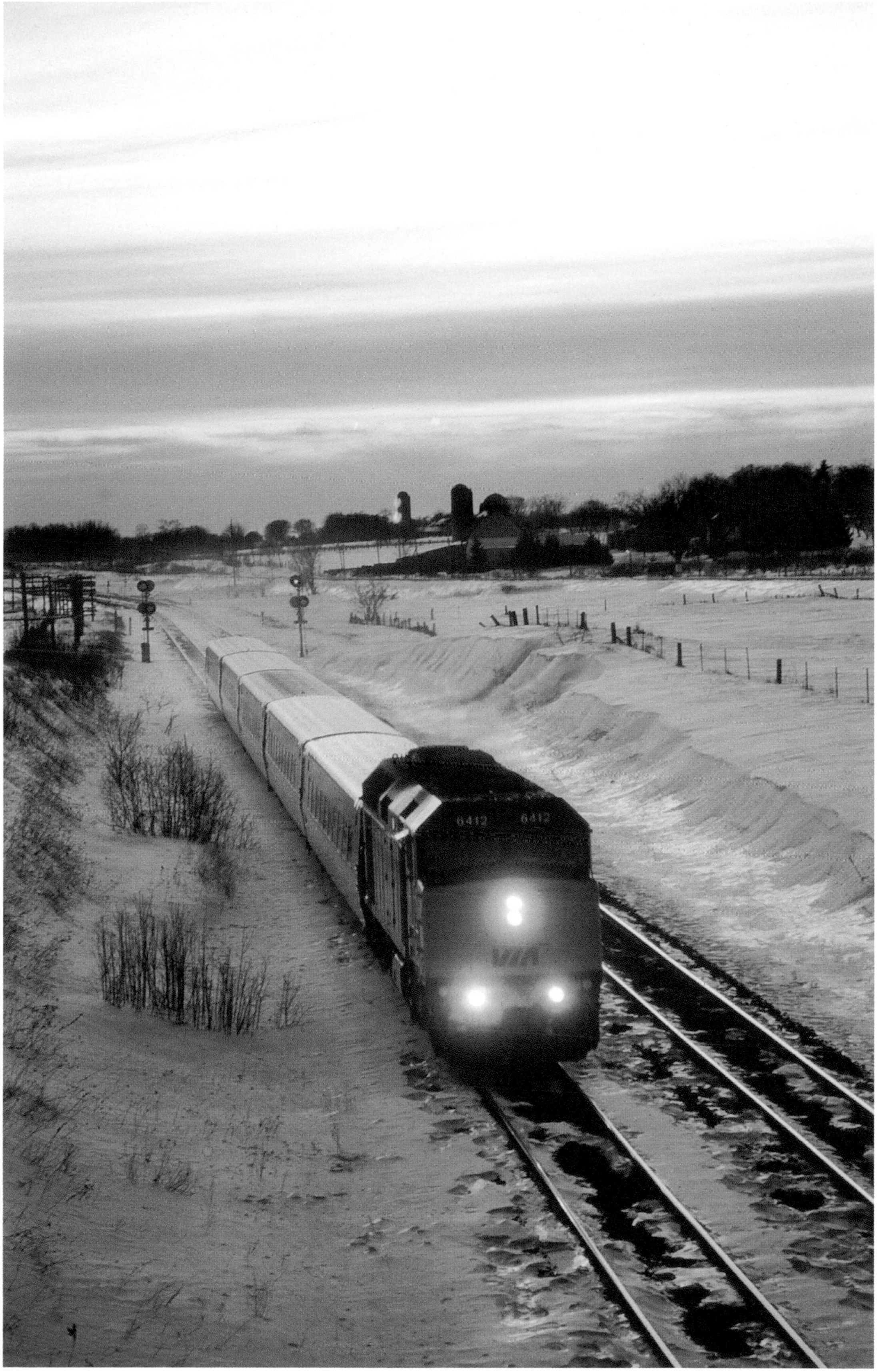

The "clear" signal in the opposing direction on the set of block lights that F40PH-2 No. 6412 and train have just passed indicate there is westbound traffic ahead on February 27, 1993. *John Leopard*

A CN conductor watches carefully from the platform of van No. 79907 as VIA LRC-2 No. 6916 glides past after its meet with CN freight Advance 422 near Acton, Ontario, on April 23, 1988. *Andreas Kellar*

appointed J. Frank Roberts, who was previously CN's general manager of passenger sales and services, as the first president and CEO of VIA. Garth Campbell also made his way over to the VIA Rail executive ranks as vice president of sales and marketing. Before the end of the month, all key officers were appointed and the marketing department was fully staffed; what began as a promotional idea was quickly evolving into a genuine passenger company in its own right.

By the end of March, coinciding with the cessation of CN and CP's marketing campaigns for their own passenger services, VIA had acquired all of CN's passenger equipment and as of June 1 was fully responsible for the management of passenger services formerly handled by its big brother. In anticipation of assuming responsibility for the provision of joint passenger service, VIA published the first VIA/CN-VIA/CP timetable in advance of this date. It contained a list of each railway's passenger schedules distinguishable by colored tabs along the top of each corresponding page: blue for VIA/CN and red for VIA/CP Rail, a practice that continued until the following year.

Back at the Negotiating Table

Negotiations between the government and what now were three railways continued with a reasonable amount of progress. Internal government memoranda showed that it would be easier for Parliament—for accountability and legal concerns, such as the 1955 CNR Act—if VIA were an independent Crown Corporation. Separation from the Canadian National was essential to achieve this status and would serve to simplify the relationship between CN and VIA by "eliminating the need for the unanimous shareholders' agreement otherwise required to [maintain] an arms' length relationship." The move also facilitated government subsidization of all operating expenses for VIA passenger services, which was a big concern for CN and CP alike. Nevertheless, both companies were reluctant to give up complete operational management of their respective passenger services until full cost recovery was assured and a date for implementation of the Crown Corporation was set. April 1, 1978, was tentatively selected.

The CTC was also making progress with its public hearings held nationwide in response to Otto Lang's report on the overall future of Canadian rail passenger services. Information gathered at these forums, combined with its own research, led the CTC to quickly determine that the creation of VIA and other 1976 railway policy initiatives would most likely lead to the complete subsidization of rail passenger services. With the intention of avoiding further deficit through an increase in revenue, decrease in costs, or a combination thereof, the CTC tabled four proposals directly related to the development of VIA, should it be established as a Crown Corporation. The four proposals, labeled "VIA 1" though "VIA 4," were graduated with each suggesting a greater purview than the last for the final orientation of VIA as a Crown Corporation.

The first, "VIA 1" (not to be confused with VIA Rail's present-day first-class service), suggested that VIA should become a small planning and advisory group to negotiate and monitor a government contract for the provision of rail passenger service by CN and CP. "VIA 2" was the same as the first, expanded to include the marketing of services. In the end, both were rejected because government was wary that their implementation might suggest only a partial commitment to testing the viability of rail passenger service.

A four-car consist makes up the Canadian Pacific's *Atlantic*, about to depart Montréal's Windsor Station for Saint John, New Brunswick. FP7 No. 4069 was one of four units in the motive pool on CP's Montréal–Rigaud commuter line when sold to VIA. *David Brandenburg*

"VIA 3" expanded the previous two proposals to include planning, marketing, and employing passenger service personnel. Additionally, the operation of trains and the use of assets would be accomplished through contracts with the railways. This suggestion was also rejected in favor the final proposal, "VIA 4," which incorporated the three previous proposals and included the acquisition of all passenger service assets from both CN and CP Rail, alleviating the proliferation of contractual agreements between VIA and the railways.

The establishment of VIA as a Class 1 railway and its subsequent promotion had the unexpected effect of raising public expectations that rail passenger service would be improved and expanded over the long term rather than rationalized and improved only where appropriate and on a cost-effective basis. Even before the government determined that VIA would indeed become a Crown Corporation, unionized rail passenger service employees saw VIA as a *de facto* employer of railway personnel and became stakeholders in the development of the new passenger railway. In its report to the Treasury Board on the principle options for the

The platform alongside Kingston's track No. 2 is empty and all passengers are either on board or making their way through the tunnel under the tracks to the station. FP9 No. 6518 awaits a highball before continuing east in May 1987. *Author collection*

corporate structure of VIA, Transport Canada commented on the union's view of VIA and the possibility of labor unrest during contract negotiations if VIA were to be incorporated as only a manager of passenger services rather than as an employer.

VIA's metamorphosis into a Crown Corporation reached its end phase in February 1978, by which time both CN and CP, along with representatives of railway unions, strongly supported the "VIA 4" proposal for VIA to become both an employer and an owner of assets. Government also approved and forwarded its recommendation to the Treasury Board for VIA to be placed as a Schedule "D" Crown Corporation under Paragraph 66(3)(c) of the Financial Administration Act. All that remained was Parliamentary approval, which was granted through an order-in-council. Effective April 1, 1978, VIA Rail Canada Incorporated was born.

Despite this noteworthy achievement, several important but unfinished businesses in the continued development of this publicly owned venture had yet to be dealt with. Of particular note, the purchase of high-speed LRC equipment was pending, the CTC had yet to release its recommendations on how the national passenger network would be rationalized, employee negotiations were still underway, and contracts for the purchase of assets from CN and CP were yet to be drawn up. As well, there was the method of "backdoor entry into public

Five months before VIA assumed control of the route, *The Canadian* continues its descent from the Rocky Mountains and through the foothills of the Stony Indian Reserve at Morley, Alberta, on May 28, 1978. There had been a station with agent here a little over a decade earlier, harkening to an earlier era when locals arrived trackside on horseback to watch the passing trains. Those are all memories now, and the train itself will become a memory in just 12 years time. *Robert Sandusky*

enterprise" used by government to create VIA to contend with, a shortcut that hampered the best intentions of its administrative and managerial staff to maximize the potential of the railway.

The use of an order-in-council (akin to an executive order in the United States) avoided debate by circumventing the House of Commons, and thereby kept VIA exposed to the threat of political impulse. Although the order-in-council was expedient, for the second time in the corporation's short history, the Liberal government missed the opportunity to provide VIA with its own act under which to operate. The government had permitted the creation of VIA as a Crown Corporation that was forced to function in a contradictory environment, subject to both the financial restrictions of the federal government and to the regulatory decisions of the CTC.

Following the 1978 general election, the Progressive Conservative party replaced the Liberals with a minority government and endeavored to table a VIA Rail Canada Act (VRCA) before the House of Commons. The initiative, led by Conservative Transport Minister Don Mazankowski, resulted in a flurry of activity at both Transport Canada and the CTC to generate a series of forward-thinking documents and proposals that may have benefited VIA as the next decade approached. Unsurprisingly, neither CN nor CP was content with the VRCA proposal and were loath to withdraw from the costing order that would eventually be used to charge operating expenses to VIA. Regrettably, it was a vain attempt to pass legislation

Trains inbound for Montréal's Central Station via the Mount Royal Tunnel proceed unassisted. Just prior to entering the tunnel, the engineer of VIA FP9ARM No. 6310 will ease back on the throttle to idle the locomotive and coast train 134 down the grade on June 21, 1991. After CN retired its boxcab electrics in 1995, VIA could no longer operate through the tunnel and rerouted its trains around Mount Royal, adding 10 miles (16 kilometers) to the route. *A. Ross Harrison*

as the minority government was toppled by a Liberal-led non-confidence vote over the Federal budget after a mere nine months. In a surprising upset at the polls, the Trudeau Liberals were ushered back into power with their strongest majority government to date and the VRCA bill died on the table. Unfortunately for VIA, this precarious state of affairs would persist to plague the railway in the not-too-distant future and even threaten its very existence.

Rationalization

Coinciding with VIA's formation as a Crown Corporation was the assumption of all passenger services from the railways under the provision that those considered "rationalized" by the CTC would be fully subsidized. Rationalization also included the selection of a single station in Vancouver, Winnipeg, and Montréal, which had separate terminals for each parent railway. In all three cases, the former CN building was selected. VIA would also assume responsibility for the few remaining routes awaiting a final decision from the CTC; these particular services would continue to operate under the 80 percent subsidy arrangement until their fate was decided. The rationalization process focused, in turn, on each of four sectors corresponding to the passenger services previously provided throughout the nation by both CN and CP: western transcontinental services, eastern transcontinental services, regional services, and remote and essential services. The rationalization of each was targeted for

Sceneramic dome No. 2403 *Fraser* in its regular midconsist assignment on the CN's *Super Continental*. One of six of the type acquired by the Canadian National in 1964, the *Fraser* is being attended to by a trainman at Jasper, Alberta, while father and son look on. *CN photo, Coo/West collection*

VIA/CN FPA-4 No. 6765 and an unidentified F9B have just left the turntable of the Spadina roundhouse en route to their next assignment. Even though the construction of the SkyDome stadium (now Rogers Centre) following Spadina's closure has long since replaced the sights, smells, and sounds of railroading with those of popcorn, hotdogs, and baseball, the 6765 survives in quiet splendor at Exporail in Delson, Québec. *Ian McCord collection*

completion by the end of March 1979. Ultimately, what remained of both eastern and western transcontinental services was more or less a continuation of what had existed prior to the formation of VIA.

The Canadian and the *Super Continental* were retained in the West while, out East, the *Ocean* and *The Atlantic* rolled on following the discontinuation of CN's *Scotian*. Regional services were also effected with the elimination of several mixed and short-haul trains. These changes paled in comparison to the CTC's initial recommendations, particularly in western Canada, where they suggested the replacement of portions or, in some cases, the entirety of overnight transcontinental trains with daytime services.

Described as the "preferred" of three potential choices for the Canadian West, the CTC advocated a single transcontinental

VIA's only road unit, RS-10 No. 8558, joins the motive power team for the September 8, 1979, consist of the eastbound *Canadian*. Two cars back from the locomotives, the 24-duplex roomette I-series sleeper, distinguishable by its 12 staggered windows and 6-wheeled trucks, was one of 20 built by the Canadian Car and Foundry for the CNR in 1950. Often used as crew dormitories by VIA, six were converted to *Dayniter* coaches in 1976 while the remainder were retired by 1983. *Richard Yaremko*

train without sleeping- or dining-car amenities to operate west of Winnipeg. All remaining services would be provided through an intercity network of self-powered rail diesel cars (RDCs) and LRCs. Although the use of LRCs in the prairies might seem odd after 25 years of service unique to the Corridor, government, for a time, had intended to operate them in western Canada. It was thought that LRC consists, in place of overnight transcontinental trains, would achieve a "substantial reduction in . . . rapidly escalating rail passenger deficits" and the replacement of one transcontinental with day trains would save $55 million annually, eclipsing the cost of new equipment within two years.

The initial purchase of three LRC train sets was seen by government as a cost-saving measure for transcontinental services and unprofitable regional services in the Maritimes. Otto Lang responded to these expectations by increasing the total number of LRC train sets purchased to 10. At one point, the acquisition of an additional 500

Given that VIA's two E8As, Nos. 1800 and 1802, were assigned to the *Canadian* over CP trackage, each was renumbered to 1898 and 1899, respectively, in October 1980 to avoid confusion with numbers assigned to CP's RS-18 fleet undergoing rebuild at the time. *Coo/West collection*

LRC-type coaches was even discussed as a possible fleet replacement standard due to the "domestic advantage" of their all-Canadian manufacturer but it never came to pass.

Despite the CTC suggestion for restricted transcontinental services, VIA assumed control of the CP's *Canadian* and the CN's *Super Continental* on October 29, 1978, and by April 1, 1979, rationalization of all Canadian passenger services by the CTC was condensed into a set of 41 Subsidiary Service Requests. By the end of the month, Dr. Bandeen resigned as chairman to permit the appointment of someone from outside CN's executive, and the Canadian government purchased all 52,000 shares of VIA Rail to become the sole shareholder. With this, VIA's charge over rail passenger services in Canada was complete and the railway, with its substantial fleet of motive power and rolling stock acquired in advance of becoming a Crown Corporation, would press onward into the next decade.

Filling the Coach Yard

VIA's potential for equipment acquisition from its parent railways included a substantial fleet of motive power and rolling stock that offered a diversity of amenities and mobile architecture. The register of equipment originally made available for sale to VIA amounted to a staggering 952 passenger cars, 92 RDCs, and 148 locomotives, not including the LRCs yet to be built. Actual procurement numbers would be smaller and by 1980 VIA reduced its fleet further through the retirement of antiquated equipment. Aside from the ex-CN *Tempo* equipment and the *TurboTrain*, the average age of this amalgamated passenger car fleet exceeded 20 years, but the railways profited directly and indirectly from the sale of this aged equipment. The transfer of ownership of this equipment to VIA Rail created an indirect profit for CN and CP as removal of these cars from their rosters yielded a significant savings in maintenance and operation costs. More directly, the CTC Rail Transport Committee's reconciliation of the equipment sale reported a financial gain of $15 million by CP Rail. However, because of its measured withdrawal from rail passenger service over two decades and subsequent reduction in related equipment, CP sold a much smaller collection of rolling stock to VIA than did its publicly owned competitor.

The limited increase in passenger traffic during 1967 marked the final appearance for a great majority of CPR passenger trains and following the centennial rush the number of passenger cars on the CPR roster dropped dramatically. By 1972, virtually all of CP's heavyweight equipment would be retired or sold and in many cases scrapped, precluding some of the railway's more interesting rolling stock from making it to VIA Rail. All 19 U-series tourist sleepers refurbished to match the stainless steel *Canadian* succumbed to

Following the practice of the original CPR *Canadian*, VIA train No. 2 will split into two sections at Sudbury, Ontario, on the morning of August 29, 1986. The larger section will continue on to Ottawa and Montréal as train No. 1 while the smaller set, led by FPA-4 No. 6780, will head south for Toronto as train No. 10. This practice differs slightly from when Canadian Pacific operated the *Canadian* as trains 1 and 2. For the CP, the Toronto–Sudbury section was numbered trains 11 and 12, respectively. *André Menard*

Carrying a set of kerosene markers on the rear of a two-car set of Budd cars, VIA RDC-9 No. 6005 takes on passengers at CP's West Toronto station. The 6005 was one of seven CN had purchased from the Boston & Maine in 1965. The lack of cab windows beside the diaphragms is a feature that denotes this unit as a passenger-only RDC-9. *Coo/West collection*

the latter fate. The few heavyweights that survived the torch were pressed into auxiliary service as accommodation cars for maintenance-of-way personnel.

CP's complement of smooth-sided lightweight passenger cars fared better than their heavyweight cousins. With the exception of the 14 *Grove* series and the four ex-NYC *Dale* series 10-5 sleepers that were sold and scrapped, the greater part of this rolling stock was included in the sales quote to VIA. The lightweight equipment that was ultimately purchased from the CP comprised a group of 15 2200-series coaches and 13 baggage cars from the 2400 and 2700 series, but these would be retired within two years due to financial constraints and compatibility concerns with the rest of the VIA fleet.

Although somewhat threadbare on the interior after a decade of inattention, VIA's premier acquisition from CP was their inventory of 169 cars built by the Budd Company of Philadelphia for the 1955 *Canadian*. Initially, ex-CP equipment was overshadowed by the large quantity of ex-CN rolling stock on VIA Rail's roster. However, by the end of the next decade, the corrosion-resistant properties of the stainless-steel Budd equipment had outlasted its counterparts of CN heritage.

Equipment made available for new ownership by CN would form the dominant share of VIA Rail's rolling stock, reflecting the

CN's more active approach to rail passenger services. Documents of sale and transfer from the publicly owned railway reveal an aggregate figure of some 737 passenger cars comprising 38 different types of accommodation configurations. This assortment included, but was not limited to, 13 types of club and/or lounge cars, 12 separate versions of sleeping cars, 10 coach/*Dayniter* configurations, and a cluster of dining and meal service cars.

Among the more interesting equipment to make its way from CN to VIA were the full-length dome cars that CN had obtained in an equipment purchase from The Milwaukee Road in 1964. These six "Sceneramic" domes were initially leased by the railway and were frequently utilized on the western leg of the *Super Continental.* The CN–Milwaukee Road transaction also included a sextet of unique sleeper-lounge-observation "Skyview" cars that unfortunately did not last until the conception of VIA. After refurbishment, CN named the cars for famous bays in the Maritimes and saw service on the tail end of the Montréal–Halifax *Ocean*. A CTC decision in the early 1970s founded on concern over lack of an emergency exit at the rear of the car caused the withdrawal of the Skyview units. All six languished in the Winnipeg coach yard until their disposal in 1977.

Motive Power

Both railways provided a measure of railway heritage in their sale of almost 150 cab units to VIA Rail, resulting in one of the largest fleets of its kind in North American revenue service. For more than a decade after the nationalization of rail passenger services, this inheritance of railway history was the mainstay of motive power and could be seen leading trains to and from all three Canadian coastlines. The vintage units also drew the attention and admiration of railfans from across North America.

The most prevalent and sturdiest cab units VIA acquired were a collection of General Motors FP7s and FP9s in both A- and B-unit configurations, manufactured in GM's Electro-Motive Division factories between 1952 and 1958. VIA would rebuild these locomotives several times throughout their service careers, the most notable of which were the conversion of ex-CP FP7s to FP9 standards and the selection of 15 FP9s for remanufacturing in the early 1980s with the designation FP9ARM. These units remained in revenue service a decade longer than any other F units on the railway.

CN's motive power contribution was no less auspicious. In 1958, the Montreal Locomotive Works introduced a cab unit version of its RS-18 road switcher. That

Gracefully navigating the S curve near O'Brien, Ontario, RDC-2 No. 6205 and RDC-4 No. 6250 have almost reached their destination of White River, Ontario, in the fading daylight of October 11, 1994. The all-baggage 6250 is indeed a rarity, the last remaining RDC-4 in revenue service of 14 built for Canadian railways. *John Leopard*

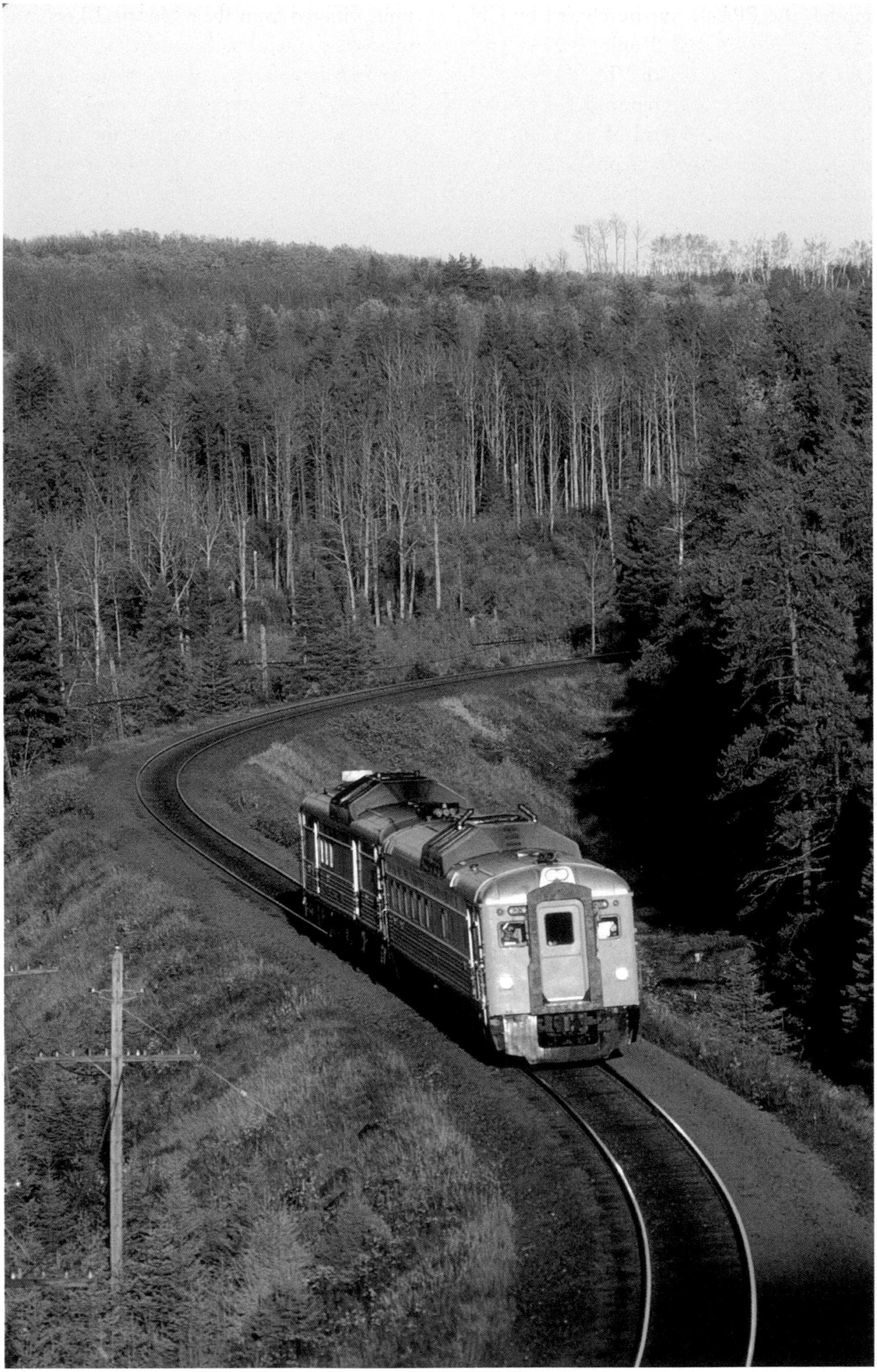

model, the FPA-4, was purchased by CN, again in both A- and B-unit arrangements. During their career with VIA, the 44 units in this series served predominantly in the Corridor and at the head of VIA's intercity trains and on eastern transcontinentals while others of that class were often assigned to the Toronto–Sudbury and Montréal–Sudbury legs of the *Canadian*.

The original motive power roster also included numerous oddities that remained in VIA Rail service until 1982. Three E8As delivered to CPR in 1949 were the only ones of their kind purchased by a Canadian railway. Two of this trio made their way to VIA (the third wrecked during the late 1960s) and frequently led the *Canadian* for several years. Both E units sometimes shared this assignment with the sole road switcher acquired by VIA, also from CP: No. 8558, an RS-10 built by MLW in 1956. CN also passed along a quartet of unique locomotives in the form of two FPA-2s and two FPB-2s. Identical to the FPA-4s internally, these four units differed from their Montreal Locomotive Works–built cousins in that they lacked a grille below the louvers on the after-end of the locomotive. Additionally, a single FPA-2, No. 6758, was one of only two units known to have received the application of a blue VIA logo on its nose in place of the standard red one, the other being FPA-4 No. 6775.

Self-Propelled Equipment

The rail diesel car (RDC), commonly referred to as a Budd car, was introduced by the Budd Company in the late 1940s as a means for railways to reduce operating costs. Perhaps described as simply a self-propelled coach, offered in several passenger- and baggage-carrying configurations, their use was considered to be less expensive than a traditional consist of a locomotive and passenger cars. RDCs were placed into service on the CNR as "Railiners" in the early 1950s and promoted as "Dayliners" on the CPR by mid-decade. The companies used RDCs on both low- and high-density routes of various

Among the victims of the 1990 service cuts were several RDC locals, whose schedules provided a form of commuter service into both Toronto and Montréal. Viewed from the southeast corner of the Don Valley Brick Works during a July evening in 1985, the Toronto–Havelock RDC local crosses the CP Rail's Don Branch viaduct over the Don River and CN's Bala Subdivision. *Andreas Kellar*

distances and eventually even on commuter services. By the late 1970s when VIA amassed its passenger fleet, a significant portion of this roster comprised five different Budd car configurations and a refurbishment program was detailed for all 96 RDCs in VIA's 1978 budget outline to the Treasury Board.

The set of cars acquired from CN provided a slightly greater variation in configurations than those of the CP. While both railways contributed numerous all-coach RDC-1s and coach-baggage RDC-2s, fewer mail-express/coach-baggage RDC-3s were obtained since Railway Post Office services had concluded in Canada in 1972. Both railways converted many of their RDC-3s to RDC-2 standards. Next on the VIA roster was the mail-express/baggage RDC-4, unique among

It is difficult to forget the sturdy and purposeful profiles of MLW FPA-4s that had a shorter life with VIA than did their GMD partners. However, some have gone on to third careers with tourist operations around North America. Looking a bit work-worn but with a shiny nose is FPA-4 No. 6775 with matching B unit 6871, rocketing along the Oakville Subdivision at Lorne Park with VIA train 73, the *Trilllum Rapido*, on Christmas Eve Day, 1981. Even in the early 1980s, some rolling stock has yet to be repainted in VIA livery. *Robert Sandusky*

Budd cars as it was shorter in overall length and carried no passengers. As with the RDC-3s, the mail compartments were removed from these units. The RDC-5s, referred to as RDC-9s by the CNR, carried only passengers but could not operate on their own. Although they were fitted with a drive motor, they had no cab for an engineer and had to be coupled with another RDC.

Even though the large majority of VIA's fleet was aged, its diversity offered more than just an auspicious start. VIA had at its disposal the tools, the talent, and enough support from government to launch itself as a successful passenger venture into the 1980s. Before long, one member of this tripartite formula would withdraw, leaving VIA to fend for itself, unsupported.

On January 14, 1990, the eve of the second round of service cuts, the final edition of VIA train 607 has just arrived in Truro, Nova Scotia. A visit by this train was like the passing of the Angel of Death herself—each of the previous 14 stations from Sydney to Stellarton now lay silent, their doors forever closed to passengers. As patrons board and disembark, the service staff solemnly performs their duties in preparation for the final leg of the trip to Halifax. By first light, both lead RDC-1 No. 6137 and the trailing RDC-2 will be shunted into the dead line to await an uncertain future. *Coo/West collection*

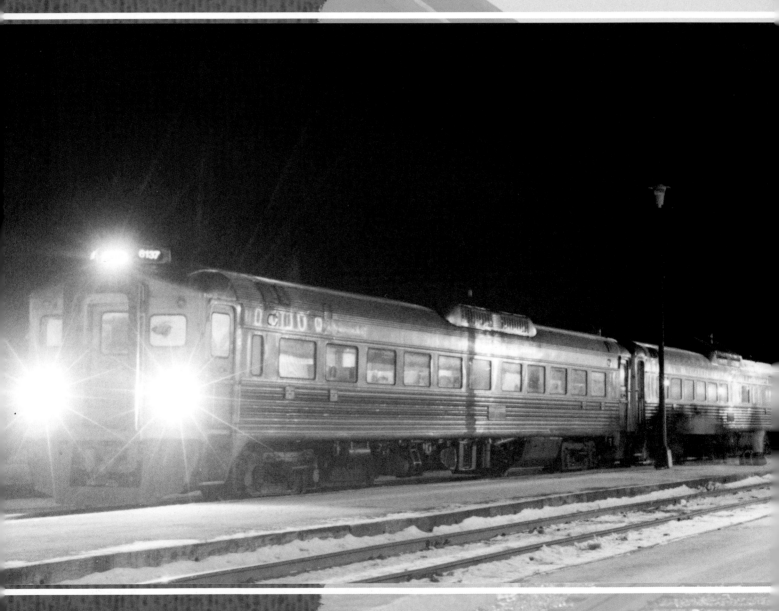

CHAPTER FIVE

THE AXE RISES AND FALLS: *1980–1990*

The 1980s were a chaotic time for the fledgling passenger railway. All that had been achieved in developing a regulated and rationalized passenger network would be significantly altered by the end of the decade. Several problems continued to plague effective development. VIA still had no official mandate and lacked specific direction from government during its formative years. What little instruction VIA

New round-trip
excursion fares

VIA/CN first offered its roundtrip excursion fares with this brochure, effective October 1, 1976. The conjoined red and blue arrows seen here were meant to represent the savings one could yield with the roundtrip excursion fare, loosely based on the Red, White and Blue fare plan. The cost was a standard one-way fare plus one-tenth, where the standard fare was represented by the blue arrow and the lesser-value fare was denoted by the red arrow. This logo was dropped and eventually used in 1977 for Terra Transport, the subsidiary cost center CN created for its Newfoundland freight operations. *Jason Shron collection*

executives did receive came in the form of conflicting signals from the CTC and the Transport Ministry. This confusion resulted in VIA developing a business plan that set goals beyond what the government was willing to commit to. In addition, equipment and cultural differences compounded VIA's difficulties. The vast transport system it inherited included antiquated equipment that was costly to maintain and employees whose embedded railway culture, including habituation to earlier styles of service and their former CP or CN operating experiences, did not adapt easily to a fast-changing transportation market. To make matters worse, VIA's attempts to overcome these disadvantages by improving services and luring passengers came under constant fire from other elements of the passenger transportation industry, led by the highway bus lobby.

Fare For All

To level the differences in fares offered by its parent railways VIA devised a new fare structure in 1979, loosely based on the Red, White and Blue system formerly used by CN. Marketed as the Fare For All plan, this first attempt by VIA at fare structuring was competitively priced, only slightly more than the overall cost of bus travel and CN's former Red, White and Blue fares, and somewhat less than rates formerly charged by CP. The plan also included two discount "excursion fare" incentives for travelers that brought on a storm of controversy.

The first excursion fare applied to single-day roundtrips, provided that the return leg departed before midnight. The second was a seven-day version of the excursion fare, similar to the one-day discount, with the return leg leaving before midnight exactly seven days after departure. These two excursion fares cost significantly less than the full-fare cost of a roundtrip ticket, by almost half in some cases. These fare reductions by a publicly subsidized railway were seen as unfair competition by the bus companies and drew the ire of their executives.

Soon after learning of VIA's aggressive rate structure, Canada Steamship Lines (CSL) President Paul Martin complained to the transport minister and the CTC. Martin was "very upset" over the "predatory rate structure" presented by Fare For All, claiming that it undermined the profit potential of CSL subsidiary company Voyageur Colonial Bus Lines, and pointing to a loss of 137,000 passengers on their routes between Québec City and Toronto. Martin's grievance was groundless since Voyageur enjoyed what essentially was a monopoly in its operating area. Clearly, he and bus company executives feared that this clever marketing of rail transportation could significantly alter the habits of travelers in the region and draw a larger share of the traveling public to VIA.

The situation escalated when the Canadian Motor Coach Association stepped into the ring, publishing a document titled "The Bus Industry vs. VIA Rail" that suggested the elimination of rail passenger service in favor of a "non-subsidized intercity bus system." Barring this, the report went on to demand that VIA charge fully compensatory rates within the Corridor, rejecting the notion that the bus industry received indirect funding by citing a 1972 CTC analysis that discounted the provision of highway infrastructure as a form of subsidy.

VIA President Frank Roberts came to the defense of the rate structure and refused to "preclude the use of imagination in such programs" to explore all possibilities that would allow VIA to tailor prices toward improved service quality and market demand. As the president of a subsidized company, Roberts was aware of the comparisons made between

City lights sparking on stainless steel were a welcome sight when dome cars from the original *Canadian* returned to one of their old haunts on April 17, 1998. Not having seen a VIA train in over eight years, the consist of the multi-domed tourist train is somewhat of an anomaly amid the splendor of the Calgary skyline. After spending the night in Calgary, the train traveled to Banff to collect some 120 passengers and continue on to Golden, where a second group, who had arrived in Golden on bus, would take the first group's place for the return to Banff. This special train ran from April 19 to 27, 1998. *Robert Sandusky*

Light flurries throughout the evening have yielded an inch or two of accumulation, creating a pristine layer of snow on the right-of-way lying before VIA FP9ARM No. 6303. The freshly plowed station platform is devoid of activity and all aboard the *Hudson Bay* are continuing north toward the shores of this train's namesake bay and are tucked in for the night. It's 1:55 a.m. in Dauphin, Manitoba, and train 93 will shortly move on, cutting fresh tracks in the snow. *Mark Perry*

those who received government funding and those within private industry. In his view, bus companies paid only a fraction of the cost to provide and maintain the highways on which they operated. He suggested that an impartial examination of public funding for VIA would illustrate a "great imbalance to the disfavor of the rail mode, which if corrected, would lead to an attractive, efficient and modern rail passenger system." In the United States, Roberts' Amtrak equivalent, Paul Reistrup, shared this opinion and responded to a similar claim by Greyhound's president that his company was not subsidized. Reistrup succinctly remarked that he had yet to see a snowplow on the highway with the name "Greyhound" on it.

Eventually Transport Minister Otto Lang and the CTC intervened, soothing the ruffled feathers of the bus companies at VIA's expense. Their ruling compelled VIA to develop a fare structure that would not use government subsidies to undercut other modes of transportation. Although VIA complied, in a letter to the transport minister, Roberts expressed his concern by saying,

Late autumn heralds earlier sunsets and by the time LRC-3 No. 6926 brings VIA train 68, the *Bonaventure*, into Kingston station on November 28, 1986, night has long since fallen. *H. W. Bonin*

"If VIA's fares are to be subject to the approval of the bus industry, I can see all kinds of conflict looming." Unfortunately for VIA, he was all too correct.

Increasing Tension

During its formative years, VIA struggled to balance demands from government and Transport Canada to reduce its subsidy levels and stand on its own feet with CTC rulings that continuously favored maintaining costly services. Transport Canada and the CTC were well aware of this disparity but there is little evidence to suggest any efforts by either party to assuage this problem. Instead, for reasons unknown other than an apparent malfeasance, civil servants within government and the CTC forestalled instructional correspondence intended for the railway and in some cases prevented VIA from receiving any direction whatsoever. A prime example concerned Transport Canada's attempt to convey to the CTC a deficit reduction target of 35 percent for the passenger railway. Instead of presenting the message directly to the CTC, it was made by way of a submission to the presiding Liberal cabinet. Although the CTC should have relayed this communiqué to VIA, it instead declined to even accept the instruction because it was presented to them indirectly. The situation was utter nonsense. The Transport Ministry had no choice but to relay the information through cabinet because the legal relationship between Transport Canada and the CTC precluded direct instruction and the use

For a brief period in 1980, VIA FP9 No. 6532 and two coaches, Nos. 5558 and 5590, received an experimental grey-and-yellow paint scheme in an attempt to match an early artist's rendition of how the yet-to-be-delivered LRC equipment might be painted. Similar to that applied to the prototype LRC locomotive and coach, the livery tested by VIA used yellow bands instead of the red bands seen on both the after-end of the prototype locomotive and that around the vestibule area of its coach. The VIA example also included a second yellow band around the blind end of each coach and the application of a small VIA logo overtop the men's lavatory on the side of each car. Seen here without her matching coaches, the 6532 pauses briefly with her train at the Dorval station on August 9, 1980, before continuing on the remaining 12 miles (19 kilometers) to Montréal's Gare Centrale. *Earl Roberts collection*

of a policy directive would constitute "undue interference" with the CTC and be "subject to legal challenge." The end result was that VIA did not receive the message at all.

The situation was further exacerbated by conventions made among government, CN, and CP during the negotiation process that created VIA Rail, which prevented VIA from auditing its own finances. In essence, VIA was given responsibility for providing rail passenger service without the corresponding authority to control costs, yet it was expected to reduce costs and subsidy reliance.

The preponderance of costs charged to VIA Rail were generated by CN and CP to pay for trackage rights and other support services rendered. These followed a "cost-plus" formula loosely based on the same costing

order, R-6313, used to calculate the 80 percent formula that has never been made public. Interestingly enough, although subsidy funding was received from Transport Canada, charges for operational expenses were billed through the CTC—the same agency that mandated VIA to maintain chronically unprofitable passenger services instead of permitting reasonable discontinuances.

It has been suggested that VIA's inability to view expenses charged by the railways was a leading cause of increasing subsidies. Two internal CN memos lend credence to this possibility. The first, dated July 6, 1978,

VIA FPA-4 No. 6786 idles the night away with steam-heated equipment at Ottawa's Union Station on February 26, 1989. *A. Ross Harrison*

As the waning September sun glistens off the sides of cars in the Toronto dead line, a solitary stainless-steel car stands out. One of six Green series sleepers the CN purchased in 1966 and transferred to VIA 10 years later, she is a victim of the 1981 cuts and has rolled her last revenue mile in Canada. *Helmut Ostermann photo, author collection*

states that there is no surprise "to see that [CN] is being constrained by costing order R-6313." The second, dated after VIA had become a Crown corporation on May 1, 1980, states that since VIA had become an annual customer and was "billed on an actual basis, it is important that we recover our true costs." Whether the railways were disingenuous toward VIA in their invoicing remains to be seen. What is certain, however, was that the operating subsidy to VIA Rail had skyrocketed 81 percent from $232.4 million in 1979 to $422.3 million in 1981. In hindsight, the accuracy of these figures and the decisions made by the federal government and the CTC at the time based on these numbers is curious given that the reconciliation of VIA's accounting and the expenses charged by CN and CP were tardy, to say the least. The job of verifying and re-auditing VIA's annual expenses and reports fell to the CTC's Rail Transport Committee Railway Economy Analysis Branch, which, due to a shortfall in manpower, was late in finalizing its reports by, in some cases, several years. In fact, the CTC audit of VIA's figures between 1978 and 1981 was not completed until 1983—two years after the 1981 service cuts. As the findings became available, billing discrepancies from the railways to VIA pit the CTC against CN and CP for resolution. Most significant were alleged $3.9 and $15 million profits, respectively, in the sale of passenger equipment and motive power to VIA that remained contested by both railways and unresolved into the late 1980s.

A seldom discussed factor that exacerbated VIA's financial problems came in the form of labor protection designed to insulate union workers hired by VIA or transferred from CN and CP "from the costs and risks of passenger train restructuring." Deliberations in 1978 over the future of rail passenger policy for VIA included a requirement for the transport minister from cabinet to develop measures within the new policy that would "assist railway employees adversely affected

Nighttime at the Spadina coach yard is by no means quiet. Workers bustle about the fleet to clean, maintain, and prepare the next day's trains in May 1985. *Andreas Kellar*

by service rationalization." The government generously afforded lifetime labor protection payments to union workers if VIA was forced to eliminate their jobs and they remained unemployed. This placed an extreme level of financial duress on the railway while ensuring financial security for a labor movement that for the time being would seldom mobilize in the face of service cuts.

VIA was also plagued by divisiveness among its operating regions. In 1978, VIA's management structure was divided into four regional headquarters: VIA Ontario in Toronto, VIA West in Winnipeg, VIA Québec in Montréal, and VIA Atlantic in Moncton. The late Bill Coo, who is best known for his series of scenic guides to VIA routes and as an accomplished railway photographer, worked for VIA, CN, and CP at different times over several decades and experienced the problem firsthand.

In the early 1980s, Coo was employed at the VIA Rail Marketing Department and was in utter disbelief over how divisionism had become ingrained in every VIA region, hampering productivity and, on occasion, precluding interregional efforts. One account concerned a suggestion to expand services that required an additional train to accommodate an increase in passenger demand. Upon learning of the locations that this route served, the chairperson of the meeting declined the initiative because it did not fall within his jurisdiction. Clearly, changes were needed in VIA's management system and corporate culture, but they would not be addressed until August 1983. For now, VIA had more pressing issues to contend with.

Round One

Otto Lang did not return to the portfolio of transport minister after the Liberals were elected with a strong majority government in 1980. Instead, Jean-Luc Pépin, a stated intercity bus enthusiast, was appointed. He in turn selected bus industry lobbyist Robert Tittley to sit as rail passenger administrator for Transport Canada. The deck was stacked against VIA: massive subsidy payments combined with an unfriendly political climate that was keenly aware of the much publicized discord between VIA and the bus industry.

Published descriptions of the events that led to the 1981 service cuts are inconsistent. One account claims that Pépin instructed VIA to find a way to reduce its subsidy requirement by 20 percent. This notion is partially supported by the self-published history of the Canadian Transportation Agency (the name assigned to the CTC after 1987), which claims that VIA initiated a discontinuance application in early 1981. However, a more commonly accepted version is that Pépin announced on July 27, 1981, that cabinet had exercised its power to bypass the regulatory framework of the CTC concerning rail passenger services by issuing an order-in-council to initiate service reductions of 19 percent, effective August 15, 1981, *forcing* VIA to apply for discontinuance. This decision was based on the presumption that VIA's deficit would reach $550 million by 1984, though VIA President Frank Roberts argued that $100 million of that figure was directly attributable to overcharging by CN and CP. No public hearings were held prior

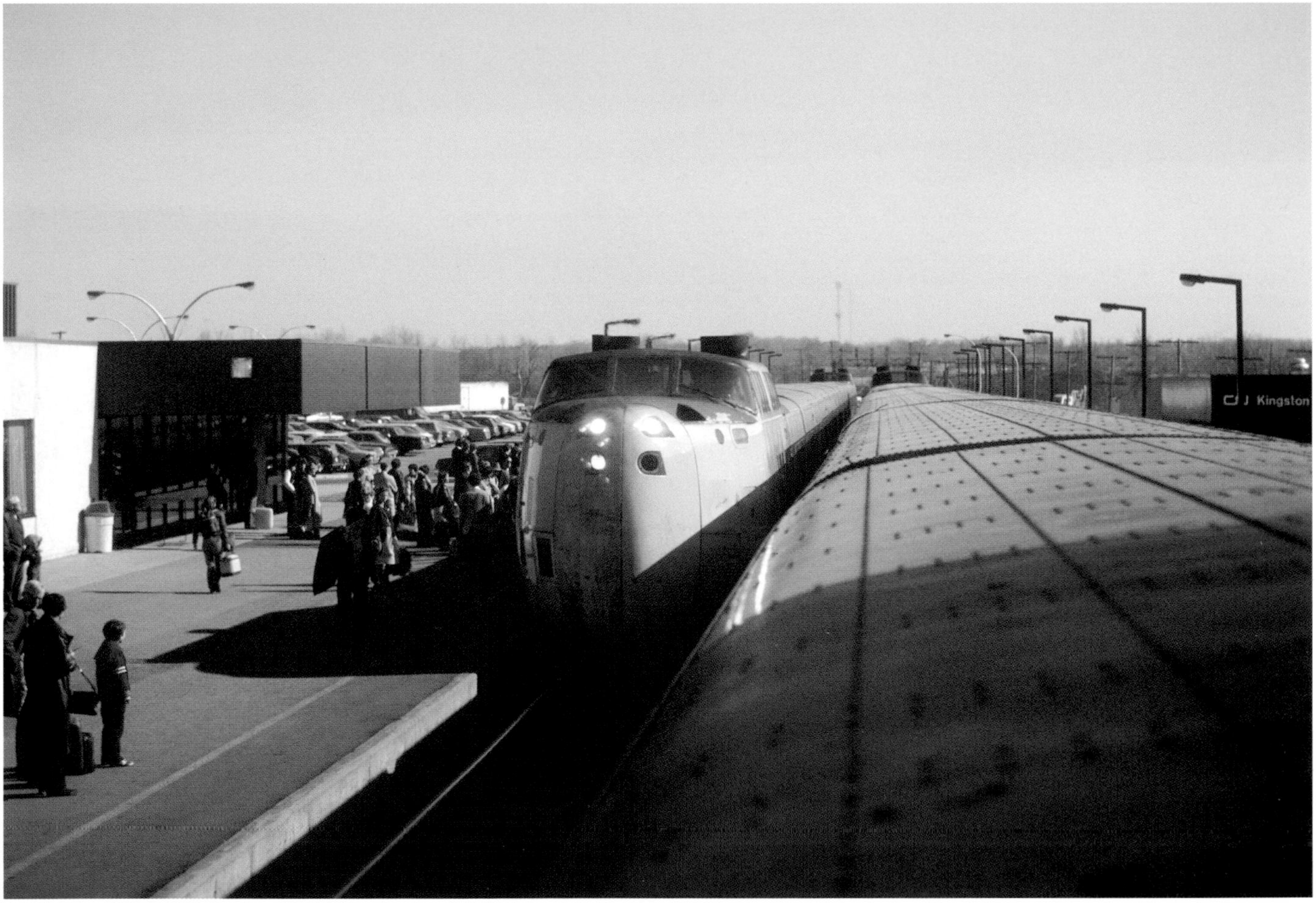

With all their tribulations notwithstanding, the *TurboTrain* power dome coaches provided a view unsurpassed by any tint-windowed Vistadome. From here, one could watch the train's almost hypnotic undulations for the entire 335 miles (539 kilometers) between Montréal's Gare Central and Toronto's Union Station. Such an experience quickly dispelled the myth induced from years of day-coach travel that this line was mostly straight and level. One could also watch the speedometer, secretly hoping to observe some yet unattained speed. Here is a peer-to-peer view of meeting east and westbound *Turbos* at Kingston, Ontario, on March 23, 1979. *Robert Sandusky*

VIA No. 132 stops at the former CPR station in Lachute, Québec, on the North Shore route between Ottawa and Montréal. Normally RDCs handled this daily run but heavier traffic on Saturday, March 24, 1979, required calling out ex-CP FP7 No. 1432 and three ex-CP 2200-series coaches. When VIA was conceived, three routes between Montréal and Ottawa had passenger train service; in 2007, only VIA's Alexandria Subdivision remains. VIA service over the CP's Lachute and M&O subdivisions, which follow the north and south shores of the Ottawa River, respectively, ended with the 1981 cuts. *Robert Sandusky*

to the service reductions and political debate within Parliament over the future of rail passenger services intensified.

Rumors of service cuts had been circulating since the previous summer when rail advocate and member of Parliament Les Benjamin leaked information obtained from sources within Transport Canada that Pépin might eliminate half of VIA services by 1984. Along with the pro-rail lobby group Transport 2000, Benjamin went on the offensive and presented research before the House of Commons that detailed a 40 percent increase in VIA ridership overall from the previous year and highlighted specific route reductions, including the Montréal–Saint John *Atlantic* that earned a 22 percent increase over the same period. Benjamin relentlessly continued his attack on what he viewed as a Liberal preoccupation with subsidy cuts to rail passenger service and claimed they "do not seem to extend to subsidies for other forms of transport." Other voices of protest would soon join the fray.

In an effort to lessen the impact of the announcement of 400 lost jobs, VIA utilized its prior knowledge of the transport minister's announcement to inform the railways and unions several days prior. The Progressive Conservatives, reintroduced to the seats

Photographed from the CN Tower in May 1982, the Spadina roundhouse and coach yard in Toronto was a major hub for VIA maintenance and operations for many years. After the closure of the Spadina facilities, VIA moved to its newly built Toronto Maintenance Centre on June 28, 1985. *Andreas Kellar*

of the official opposition after an embarrassing nine-month tenure as the ruling party, were also aware of imminent service reductions prior to the official broadcast. Further politicizing the issue, Progressive Conservatives seized the opportunity to lambaste the Liberal strategy for VIA Rail by holding 15 days of nationwide public hearings and publishing their findings in a document titled "The Last Straw: Report of the Task Force on Rail Passenger Service." Don Mazankowski led the task force, which demanded that Pépin immediately rescind the order that "emasculated" Canada's transportation services.

The Conservatives' report contained many salient and legitimate arguments that should have compelled the Liberals to reverse course, and pointed out that the use of an order-in-council to eliminate services seriously impaired the role of the CTC as protector of the public interest. Furthermore, the report implied that the Liberals had long favored the air industry, citing the Mirabel Airport fiasco and aviation subsidies of $1.5 billion in terminal services and $700 million in fuel for 1980 alone.

After the reduction announcement by Pépin, political concern over the provision of rail passenger services had become almost electric in intensity, creating prime opportunity for policy reform, and perhaps even the legislation of a VIA Rail Canada Act. However, the government chose to ignore this possibility and on November 15, despite powerful opposition, the cuts to VIA services went ahead as planned. *The Atlantic* and the *Super Continental*, along with myriad other regional services, rolled quietly on their last

Four *Superliner* cars and an F40PH locomotive leased from Amtrak during the fall and winter of 1984–1985 were tested on VIA's *Panorama* between Winnipeg and Edmonton. With VIA Tempo Electric Generator No. 15301 bringing up the markers, this train set was caught approaching Portage La Prairie, Manitoba, by the author (seven years old at the time), his four-year-old brother, and their father in October 1984. *Tom Greenlaw*

revenue miles from station platforms all across Canada.

The Canadian public, who embraced rail passenger service, viewed the government's decision as a travesty. Although federal subsidy payments had inflated beyond all expectations, VIA had successfully increased ridership and passenger miles on the majority of its 13,244 miles (21,282 kilometers), rationalized by the CTC just months before to an "irreducible minimum." This growth in ridership in the face of seemingly insurmountable odds was completely obliterated by the forced reduction in service. VIA would never recover from this loss in ridership; for this reason alone, this example of government meddling in the day-to-day operation of a Crown agency would prove to be the most devastating in VIA Rail history.

As a direct result of the cuts, a considerable amount of rolling stock was forcibly retired. A VIA operations memo written two months prior to November 15 shows some 200 cars slated as unserviceable or surplus to VIA's requirements, including the five-car *Champlain* train set and all six Sceneramic

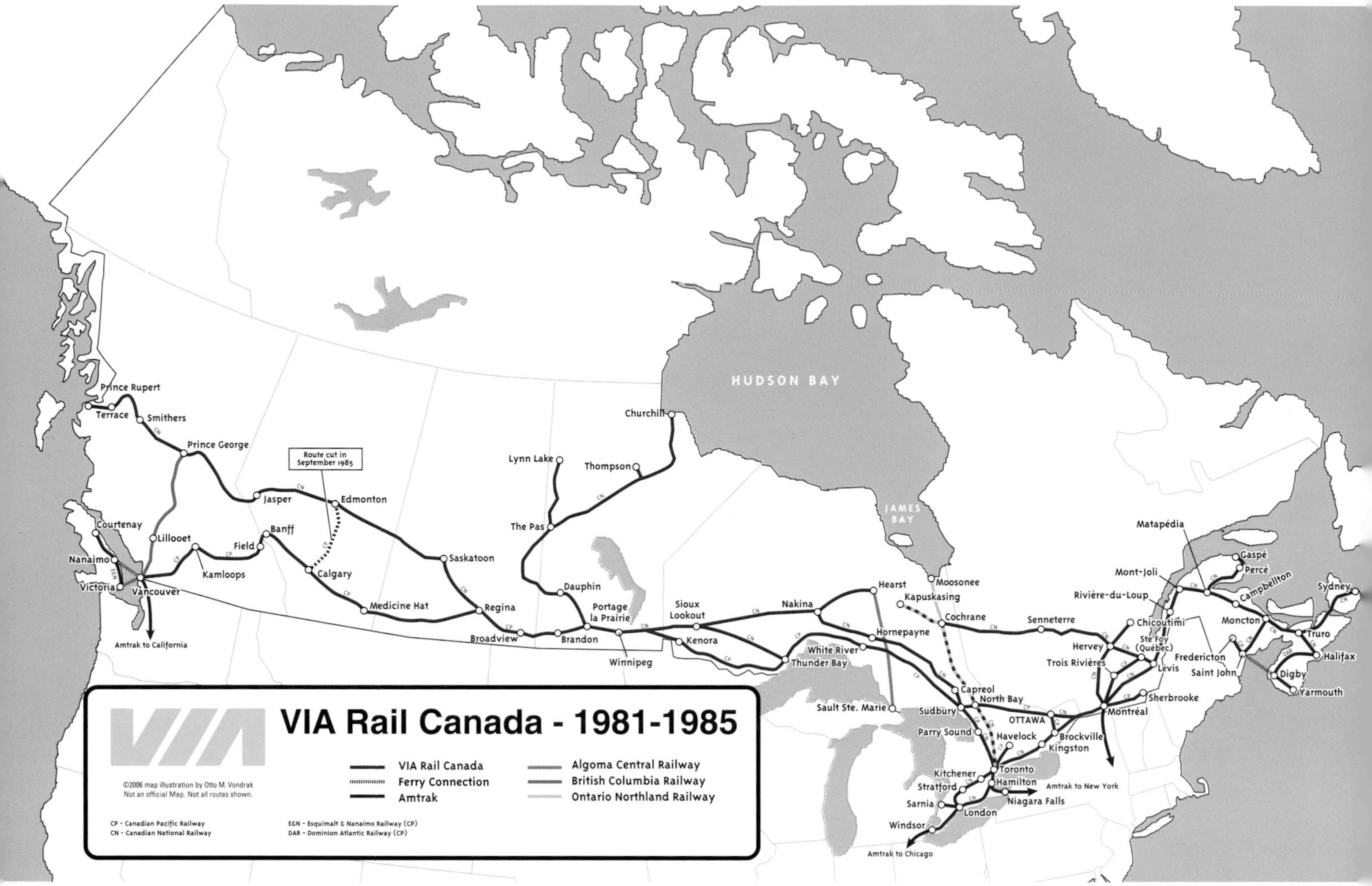

domes. Gone too were the majority of *Cape*, *Falls*, and *River* series sleeping cars. The *TurboTrain* was also retired for several reasons, most of which had to do with rising repair costs. The financial restrictions placed on VIA following the service reductions coincided with the introduction of the LRC in 1981 and the culmination of a nine-year service contract for the *Turbo*. The face of the railway was forever changed with the disappearance of this equipment from the VIA roster.

Aftermath

If it was the government's intention to strike VIA down with the sword of legislation in favor of other forms of passenger transport, the wound was not fatal. The imaginative potential of VIA employees, to which Frank Roberts had alluded, would begin to flourish in the wake of the service cuts. Meanwhile, the Liberal government carried out damage control by ensuring that a government official of some standing was present at most VIA events. Several service reinstatement ceremonies resulted from CTC recommendations to retain 15 of the original 21 axed services, and government attendance and encouragement was an attempt to pass these "inaugural" trips off as Liberal pro-rail initiatives. Further efforts to sway disgruntled voters in the years following the VIA cuts saw the replacement of Jean-Luc Pépin as minister of transport in 1983.

The long-awaited debut of the LRC was a happier milestone for VIA. Following seven

An abundance of holiday travelers heading east to the Maritimes is evident by the green markers on the nose of FPA-4 No. 6770. In accordance with Operating Rule 20, two green flags by day and two green lights by night, indicate that this consist of *The Atlantic* is the first of two sections to pass through Brownville Junction, Maine, during the early morning hours of December 23, 1980. After taking on fuel and water, it will continue east to arrive in Saint John by nine in the morning and Halifax late that afternoon. *George Pitarys*

months of trials in the Montréal area, the first train set was delivered on July 1, 1981, to the Canadian Pacific's Windsor Station in Montréal and entered revenue service in the Corridor two months later, rather than in western Canada or the Maritimes as proposed some years earlier. Windsor Station itself was closed that November when VIA chose to consolidate its services at CN's Central Station two blocks away.

Recuperation

In 1983, purpose-built maintenance facilities for LRC equipment opened in Montréal, just prior to the delivery of a second batch of LRC equipment and coinciding with VIA and Bombardier maintenance officials overcoming difficulties experienced with the LRC's hydraulic tilting system.

New Minister of Transport Lloyd Axworthy was more supportive of rail passenger transport than his predecessor and led several programs to channel money back into VIA Rail. Axworthy was able to reverse course on the government's former agenda as unrelated controversy focused public awareness elsewhere. As the LRC program was coming on-line within the Corridor, Axwor-

Not unusual for a July 1978 consist, VIA FPA-4 No. 6791 leads a mix of liveries on its four-car train. Given that the engineer has opened the door on the nose of 6791, it must be a scorcher of a day. *Author collection*

thy turned his attention to transcontinental services. The steam-heated transcontinental passenger fleet was expensive to operate and maintain, and by this time was almost 30 years old. Studies for a replacement began to circulate in early 1984 and by September VIA leased a single F40PH locomotive and a four-car set of mechanically heated and air-conditioned *Superliner* equipment from Amtrak. Two phases of testing took place over a six-week period during the fall and winter of 1984–1985 on the newly inaugurated *Panorama* between Edmonton and Winnipeg. Funding was also provided to finally construct maintenance facilities in Montréal, Toronto, Winnipeg, and Halifax, reducing costs by alleviating the need to contract maintenance services with other railways.

While beneficial for VIA's future, these changes had minimal value in the fickle public eye. Polls throughout 1983 and 1984 elicited increasingly negative public opinions that projected imminent defeat for the Liberals at the ballot box. Pierre Trudeau resigned in an attempt to improve the party's fortunes under different leadership, but to no avail; the Canadian electorate was already thoroughly disillusioned with his government.

In 1984, the Liberals suffered the biggest defeat in party history when a landslide victory handed the largest majority government in Canadian history to the Progressive Conservatives under Brian Mulroney, whose campaign incidentally included promises to restore several VIA Rail services. Over the next eight years, Mulroney's politics would

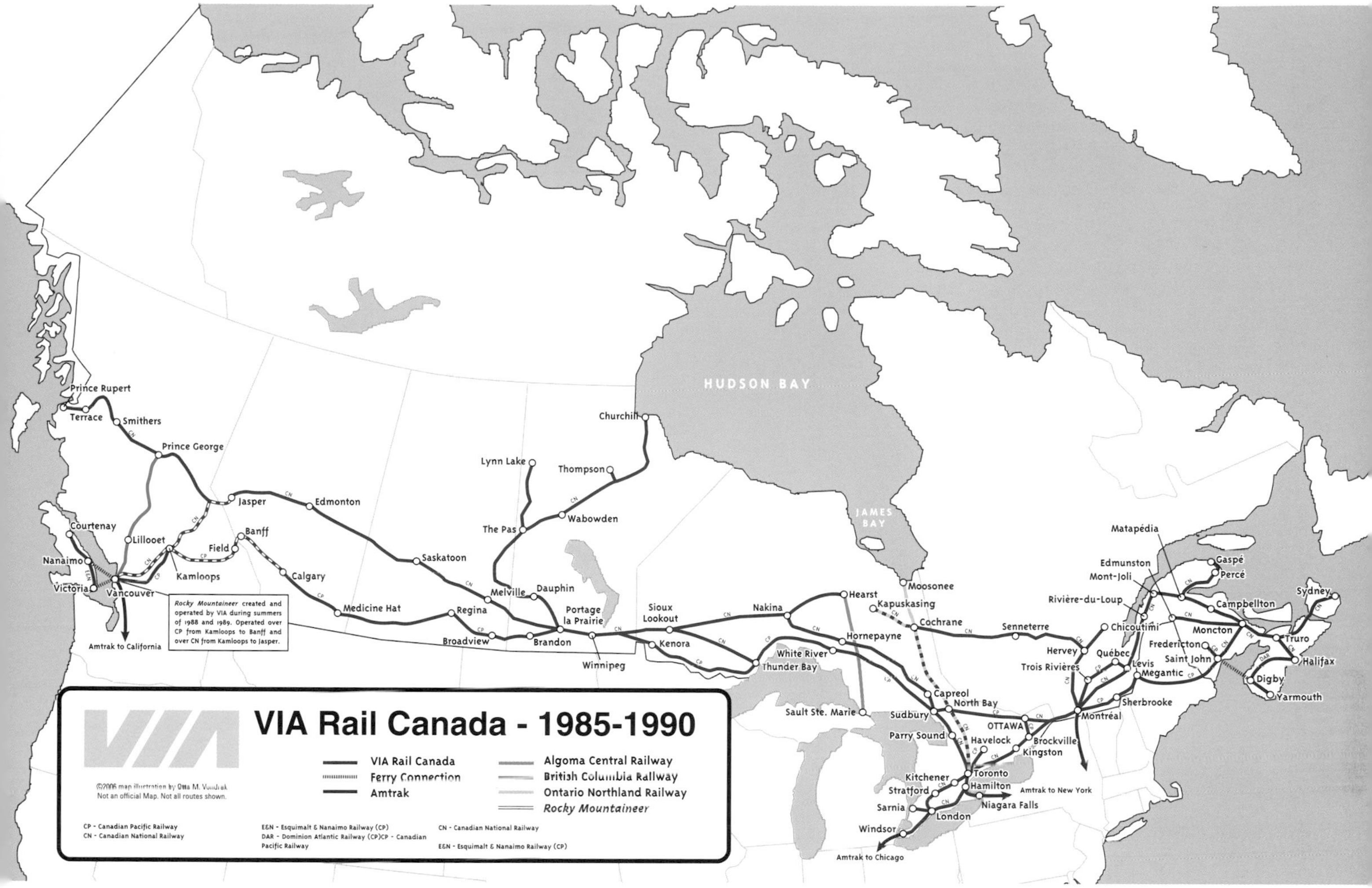

first elevate the fortunes of VIA and then ultimately crush them.

Reform

In the Conservative Cabinet, Don Mazankowski was once more appointed to the position of transport minister and with that came hope for a turnabout in VIA Rail's future. He immediately addressed the VIA issue by forming the three-member Rail Passenger Action Force to study, yet again, the future of rail passenger services in Canada and as promised, restored six VIA services, including *The Atlantic* and *Super Continental* on June 1, 1985. Mazankowski's ambition to reform the railway industry reached far beyond his desire to address the needs of VIA Rail; a brand-new Railway Act would be tabled and the CTC would receive a facelift to become the Canadian Transportation Agency (CTA).

During their years in opposition, the Progressive Conservatives relentlessly harassed the Liberals concerning their policy on VIA Rail and staunchly supported numerous proposals in favor of a VIA Rail Canada Act (VRCA). Once the Conservatives returned to power, Mazankowski made the legislation of a VRCA a priority and dusted off the drafts that had been developed by staff at Transport Canada and the CTC during his previous tenure as transport minister.

Throughout the winter and spring of 1985, the Action Force continued to deliberate and it published its findings in a letter to the transport minister on May 23, 1985. The key points of this report echoed many issues

First, a tiny light down the long tangent shimmers slightly with the changing air currents in the late-winter sunset. Then, almost noiselessly, it's upon you. Its red CN logo fading, the nine-car *Turbo* whumps past the antiquated stone mileposts that date back to when this portion of the CN line between Montréal and Toronto was owned by the Grand Trunk. Then it's gone and only the memory and the spent-fuel odor linger. ***Robert Sandusky***

of concern expressed to the CTC in previous VRCA proposals: VIA needed a formal mandate, access to invoicing and service contracts, and a new charging policy for operational expenses that would provide conditional bonuses to CN and CP for the achievement of performance standards. The report also recommended that VIA continue to improve its management structure, modernize its motive power and rolling stock based on the *Superliner* trials, and obtain all remaining CN and CP passenger assets and employees. A suggestion to present a "basic network" of service for parliamentary approval was

For the first four years of VIA's existence, the railway conducted steam excursions jointly with CN throughout the summer months from Toronto to Niagara Falls using CNR U-1-f Mountain-type locomotive No. 6060, built in October 1944. In addition to a "VIA/CN Steam Excursions" brochure published to promote the service, these fan trips were listed in VIA's system timetable. Steam excursions culminated in July 1980 with 6060 heading up two charters organized as part of the National Railway Historical Society's convention in Toronto. The first, on July 24, passes Oakville East on its last return from Niagara Falls. Assisted by VIA FP9 No. 6539 to handle the tonnage, the consist this day mainly includes VIA coaches, supplemented with NRHS member-owned private cars. *Robert Sandusky*

included along with specific directions for government and its regulatory bodies to reestablish an arm's-length relationship with all Crown agencies.

At first glance, the report could easily be interpreted as a boon for VIA Rail, given that each proposition, if successfully seen through the legislative process, would ensure the long-term feasibility of rail passenger service in Canada. A good number of these recommendations were eventually included in a Rail Passenger Transportation Act introduced to Parliament as Bill C-97 on February 24, 1986. Hailed by Mazankowski as a "dramatic new framework for VIA Rail," the act was geared toward filling the legislative gap VIA had been forced to endure by providing "greater self-sufficiency with less dependency on government funding." But alas, like the VRCA proposal in 1980, the Rail Passenger

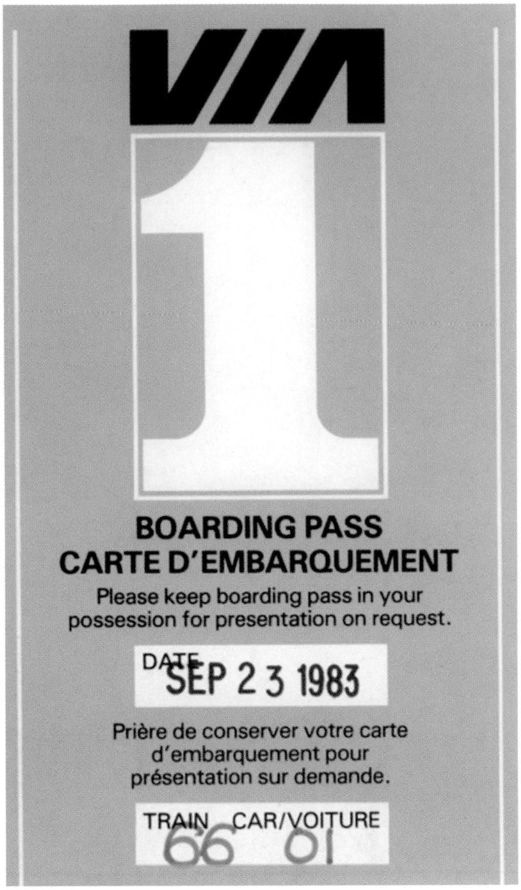
VIA
1
BOARDING PASS
CARTE D'EMBARQUEMENT
Please keep boarding pass in your possession for presentation on request.
DATE SEP 23 1983
Prière de conserver votre carte d'embarquement pour présentation sur demande.
TRAIN CAR/VOITURE
66 01

VIA-1 first-class service is introduced in the Corridor for the first time on October 20, 1980, replacing VIA's Club Service. *Author collection*

Transportation Act would also die on the order paper when Parliament was prorogued for a federal election.

All was not completely lost, however. VIA adopted numerous recommendations while the Conservatives maintained other components of C-97 in their white paper on rail transport called "Freedom to Move," a precursor to the 1987 National Transportation Act. Under this revamped policy, government established a further unofficial mandate for VIA into the 1990s. Mazankowski was first to articulate a phrase, normally attributed to then–Prime Minister Brian Mulroney, that summed up the unofficial mandate, "use it, or lose it." By the time Mulroney repeated this expression to the media some years later, the philosophy it represented was neither original nor clandestine and was well documented, starting with the report of the Rail Passenger Action Force in 1985.

Each recommendation presented by the Action Force, and in numerous iterations of the failed Rail Passenger Transportation Act, had great potential to benefit VIA. However, each benefit was subject to a specific financial performance objective to better manage government funding. Mazankowski's unofficial mandate for VIA was based on two conditions that he referred to as the "twin pillars of policy": an immediate increase in funding balanced with a budgetary ceiling of $600 million, and the reduction or abandonment of routes that failed to reach a customized revenue-to-cost and traffic ratio. The ball was thrown into the court of the traveling public; if travelers chose to frequent the train it would be just profitable enough to be maintained, or so it was thought.

Excitement before the Storm

Following the direction of government, VIA continued to implement innovative growth-oriented marketing strategies in an attempt to recapture lost passenger miles and ridership. By filling trains to capacity as much as possible, the railway would try to take control of its subsidy funding and prevent additional forced service cuts.

Measures were also taken to reduce maintenance expenses by replacing an aging fleet of first-generation cab units with 59 F40PH-2s from General Motors' Electro-Motive Division facilities in London, Ontario. The first locomotive of a three-year delivery schedule arrived on December 15, 1986. The selection of the F40PH-2 stemmed from the successful test of leased Amtrak equipment in western Canada and was the only purchase made, as the government deemed the acquisition of bi-level *Superliner* cars for use on western transcontinental trains too costly. This decision suited CP, which voiced concern on numerous occasions over the clearance of this equipment through tunnels and underneath other structures on its lines west of Calgary. The required modernization of the increasingly antiquated

Opposite: Seen near Yoho, British Columbia, a six-car, all-ex-CN coach and *Dayniter* consist make up VIA train 101, the *Rocky Mountaineer*, on August 17, 1989. *Glenn Roemer*

6401
6401
VIA

On arrival in Belleville, Ontario, the porter opens the Dutch doors of his coach, sweeps off the accumulated snow, and steps down to offer a hand to disembarking passengers. Always friendly and always smiling, so goes service aboard VIA Rail. *Coo/West collection*

fleet of passenger equipment was not overlooked, however, and in lieu of purchasing new equipment, a program to completely refurbish VIA's long-haul fleet was announced in May 1987.

Coupled with their commitment to rejuvenate the fleet, service improvements aboard VIA trains would abound: the inclusion of nonsmoking cars on Corridor trains, new uniforms for front-line staff, an improved first-class "VIA 1" service, and an "on-time policy" that awarded customers travel credits if the train arrived late at its destination, were just a few of the many fresh ideas offered to VIA customers. The railway also made its first proprietary attempt at courting the tourist-train market with the introduction of the "Canadian Rockies by Daylight" service between Vancouver and Banff/Calgary or Jasper. Drawing on experience gained in operating steam excursions cooperatively with CN in the late 1970s, daylight trips through the mountains proved so incredibly successful for VIA that it was likely the only compensatory service on the railway. Starting with 19 weekly departures in June 1988, the *Rocky Mountaineer*, as it would soon be called, brought some 17,000 visitors to the Rockies and was the mainstay of VIA's tourist packages until its forced sale to private interests two years later.

Initiatives encouraging passengers to choose VIA for their travel needs would once more become the target of bus industry executives. Voyageur Colonial Bus Lines complained to the CTA about VIA discounts in the Corridor, using the now-familiar argument that discounted fares would hurt its business and that the railway continued to have the unfair advantage of government subsidy. Again, the CTA bowed to the bus lines, ruling that discount fares were prejudicial and recommending an inquiry into VIA Rail's pricing policies. However, the inquiry was precluded by a fateful announcement in October 1989.

Round Two

The Progressive Conservative government was elected to a second term in 1988 and set about trying to reform the Canadian Constitution and ensuring that Canada was party to a North American Free Trade Agreement. As history played out, an economic recession, combined with increasing national debt, fed public scrutiny of national finances. For the

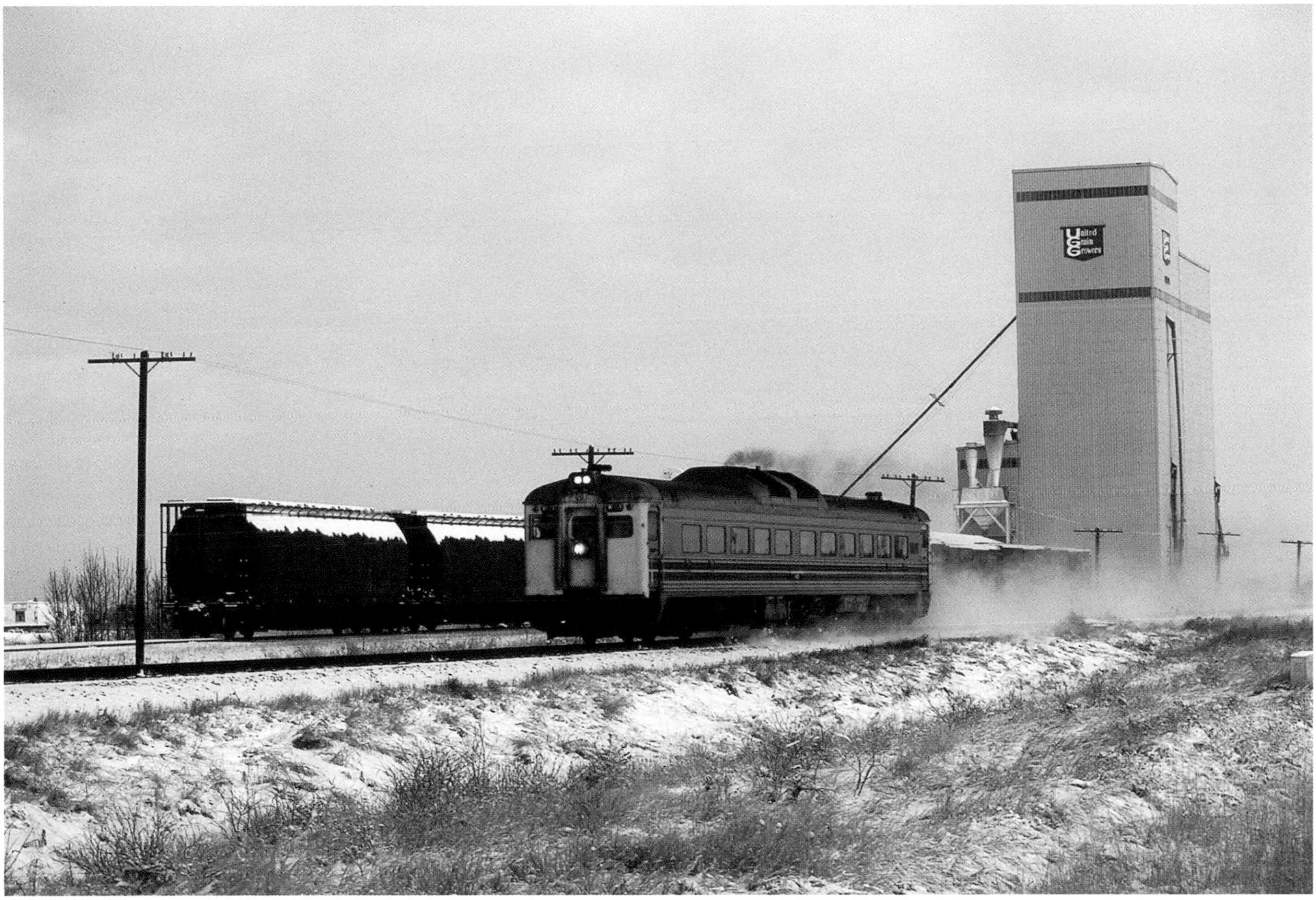

With the throttle wide open and lights fixed forward, the Edmonton–Calgary Dayliner races past a "prairie skyscraper" near Olds, Alberta, on December 12, 1981. The large Mars Light on the front door of VIA RDC-1 No. 6131 no longer oscillates as a result of a CTC decision in April 1980 determining that rotating Mars Lights and flashers on RDCs had a hypnotic effect on those running the units. The Dayliner itself was discontinued on September 7, 1985. Due to a preponderance of vehicles trying to "beat the train," federal Transport Minister Don Mazanowski cited "safety concerns" as the official rationale for canceling the route. *Richard Yaremko*

Only two months after the 1990 cuts, the dead line at Ottawa's Union Station swells with former CN passenger cars awaiting sale or scrap. *Ian McCord*

foreseeable future, government would have to significantly cut spending, or at least give the appearance of doing so. Capital subsidies flowing to the national passenger railway broke through the $600 million ceiling in 1988, breaching the first of Mazankowski's "twin pillars." VIA launched an internal study bent on fixing the subsidy issue to avoid the increasing possibility of government intervention.

Denis de Belleval, a former transport minister for the province of Québec, was appointed president of the railroad in July 1987. Upon his arrival, de Belleval applied his entrepreneurial style of management to invigorate the railway's customer service, marketing, maintenance, and operational sectors, and implemented countless improvements. Preliminary findings of the VIA study showed that an investment in high-speed rail operations within the Québec–Windsor Corridor could potentially solve the subsidy problem. De Belleval jumped onboard and tried to entice government to partake in a genuine high-speed rail project akin to those in Europe and Japan. In search of the $3 billion in funding required for the program, de Belleval pled his case to investors, financiers, and provincial and federal government bodies, explaining that the high-speed program would generate enough revenue to lessen the subsidization required for other VIA services. De Belleval's audience, however, focused on a completely different argument: the request for a further $3 billion on top of VIA's subsidy overrun.

Following the 1988 election victory, Benoît Bouchard was appointed as the Conservatives' new transport minister and his arrival at Transport Canada in November 1988 marked the beginning of a turbulent year for VIA. The difficult task of curtailing the VIA deficit would see Bouchard clash with de Belleval, whose corporate agenda differed significantly from the government's intent. The solution that de Belleval sought through high-speed rail and his extraordinary efforts to promote the railway were so enigmatic that he was viewed as a potential obstacle to the transport minister's objective.

Following a leak by the Canadian press that an announcement for a $100 million cut in the VIA Rail operating budget was

Adjacent to the Churchill, Manitoba, station and caked in snow, E-series sleeping car *Euclid* sits patiently at the after-end of train 92, the *Hudson Bay*, in February 1983. At almost the same latitude as Juneau, Alaska, Churchill is the northernmost station on the VIA network and one of seven "essential services" kept after 1990 for a town that would otherwise not have adequate access to reliable year-round transportation. *Grant Russell, Tom Greenlaw collection*

6409
6409
6409
VIA

imminent, de Belleval took a stand and paid a price. On May 3, 1989, he reportedly resigned in protest although rumors circulated that the minister of transport traveled to VIA headquarters in Montréal for the express purpose of sacking him. While at the VIA offices, Bouchard also affirmed that subsidies to VIA would be drastically reduced as part of a five-year corporate plan, from $541 million in 1989–1990 to $250 million. It would seem as though all bets were off after Bouchard's return to Ottawa later the same day. Upon being intercepted by reporters, Bouchard refused to rule out killing VIA altogether, saying that all options remained on the table and his final decision would be predicated on VIA's proposals. CN President Ron Lawless was appointed to replace de Belleval as president of VIA Rail and was given the unenviable responsibility of excising VIA routes, services, and jobs to meet government targets by the end of June 1989.

Public reaction to the forthcoming service cuts was swift. Results of a Gallup Poll published in the *Montreal Gazette* soon after the announcement showed that 80 percent of Canadians wanted Ottawa to maintain VIA Rail's existing routes, with the highest support coming from Atlantic Canada; 92 percent of Maritimers surveyed believed rail passenger service to be "very important" to their region.

As details of service reductions developed by Lawless for the Ministry of Transport began to leak out, interest groups, stakeholders, and politicians all issued separate reports countering the government's plan. Transport 2000 stepped forth and published "VIA: A Better Way" in July 1989. The document blamed VIA's poor financial performance on a lack of legislation and government's previous failures to enact the VRCA, which permitted political and bureaucratic interference and made VIA vulnerable to the vacillating whims of transport lobby groups. The report also claimed that government decision-making was influenced by experiences rather than

VIA originally conceived the *Rocky Mountaineer* tourist train before the program was sold off in 1990. Crossing the Kicking Horse River near Ottertail, British Columbia, on June 23, 1988, VIA F40PH-2 No. 6409 works its way down the grade toward Golden for only the third time during the inaugural summer of operations for the "Canadian Rockies by Daylight" service. Renamed the *Rocky Mountaineer* the following summer, the train will stay overnight in Kamloops before continuing on to Vancouver the following morning. *Ted Ellis*

Maritime rail passenger services were decimated by the January 1990 cuts, leaving only the tri-weekly *Ocean* and *Atlantic* to serve the region. No longer required, 10 RDCs languish in the dead line at VIA's Halifax station in October of the same year. *Fred Headon*

by a "coherent passenger transportation policy" and demonstrated favoritism for the aviation industry through the annual subsidy of $1.3 billion, double that received by VIA. Their solution included the provision of legislation to set attainable goals, a revised costing arrangement with the railways, and new equipment to reduce costs and attract riders.

In some ways, the service cuts Bouchard announced were like a kickoff at a football game, with VIA as the political football. The tactics the Conservatives used in 1989 to effectuate service discontinuances, providing the facade of reductions in government spending, appeared to have come from a page in the Liberal government's playbook eight years previous. The Liberals, on the other hand, played the part of the task-force jester, providing a repeat performance of the Conservatives' opposition act by arrogantly castigating the government for its policy on rail passenger services, all the while promising to restore the dignity of the railway if the public would only elect them. The same party whose cuts in 1981 decimated ridership and passenger miles on VIA insisted on the provision of a "true legislative mandate" because "the only responsible course of action is to strengthen national rail passenger services." Like the Conservative effort, the Liberals' demands had no effect on the eventual outcome.

The official announcement from Bouchard on what would become of VIA was made the following October and this second round of cuts would be far deeper than anticipated. Even the House of Commons' Standing Committee on Transport was baffled by the decision to eliminate passenger trains while so many nations worldwide continued

The Diet Pepsi "Taste Drive" train races through Carlsbad Springs, Ontario, on July 19, 1990. Between July 7 and 24, 1990, this seven-car train crossed Canada from Vancouver to Halifax over CN lines. Specially decorated for the occasion, F40PH-2 No. 6400 leads a steam generator, flatcar, diner, two *Chateau*-series sleepers, and dome-observation *Tweedsmuir Park*. *Ross Harrison*

to invest in these services. Without public hearings, and by way of order-in-council, VIA services nationwide would be sliced in half, effective January 15, 1990. Public attempts to prevent the cuts abounded in the wake of the October decision, with protesters marching in picket lines at VIA stations throughout Canada. Various stakeholders began to analyze the government's rationale and again, as in 1981, there were discrepancies and contradictory statements.

While government claimed that VIA's ridership declined 20 percent between 1981 and 1988, these calculations failed to account for the effects of the 1981 cuts. Of VIA's four transcontinental trains, the *Canadian* and the entire southern route along CP trackage was selected for elimination despite the fact that it had the highest occupancy rate in the VIA system, carrying more than a half-million people per year with a cost-recovery ratio of 48 percent, besting all but one other non-Corridor train.

As the eleventh hour approached, the Canadian Railway Labour Association (CRLA) and Transport 2000 resorted to legal action in a last-ditch effort to commute VIA's sentence. When the renegotiation of union worker contracts in 1986 altered formerly overgenerous job protection stipulations, the labor movement became a concerned stakeholder in VIA's future. The CRLA filed a motion with the CTA to request public hearings on the proposed discontinuances and asked them to investigate a breach of contract between government and the NTA in forcing a level of service far below Transportation Act requirements. In a ruling issued just 11 days before the cuts were to occur, the CTA denied the application on the

Until 1990, VIA and the Ontario Northland Railway jointly operated the overnight Northland between Toronto and Kapuskasing, Ontario. A pair of ONR FP7s lead train 128 along the Don Valley toward Toronto's Union Station on a crisp morning in March 1987. *Andreas Kellar*

basis that an order-in-council supersedes the agency's authority. Transport 2000 also made a legal claim on the grounds that service discontinuances would adversely affect the environment, but to no avail.

More than 17 services ceased to exist after January 15, 1990, when more than a hundred towns and cities saw passenger trains for the last time. Stations all across Canada were vacated, boarded up, and in some cases torn down. The most prominent service to be eliminated received a great deal of media coverage as journalists aboard the last trip of the *Canadian* broadcasted their coverage directly from the train.

The bus lobby and the opponents of rail passenger service finally accomplished what they had begun almost 40 years previous. The Canadian Bus Association and the Airline Transportation Association of Canada were openly in favor of "severe cutbacks" to VIA, insisting that successive governments' financial assistance to the railway was "patently unfair" and that rail passengers received a subsidy 14 times greater than bus patrons. Based on this "fact," transport lobbies dismissed evidence that other modes of transportation had also benefited from government assistance as "irrelevant" because VIA's subsidy levels were so large. Clearly, there was no room in the lobbyists' vision of the passenger transportation industry for aircraft and buses to include or even cooperate with rail service. VIA had to go.

One year after the 1990 round of cuts by which buses had replaced rail service in the Maritime Provinces, with the exception of the thrice-weekly Montréal–Halifax *Ocean* and the Montréal–Saint John *Atlantic*, *Halifax Daily Star* reporter Peter Hays examined the aftermath of the bus-rail struggle. Once rail services between Sydney, Halifax, and Yarmouth were cut, he wrote, the bus companies were "doing a thriving business." As buses rolled defiantly along the Maritime highways, the somber picture of 22 RDCs and a number of assorted passenger cars sitting quietly on a siding at the Halifax VIA station, awaiting sale or scrap, was seen throughout the country. Half the VIA fleet was shunted into dead lines.

Unlike the bus companies, VIA was not thriving, its network now a skeletal version of what it once was. Passenger levels during the first six months of 1990 were 55 percent less than what they had been during the same time the previous year. Travelers who were now without rail service had no alternative but to fly, ride the bus, or drive their own vehicles, and both the airlines and bus lines relished their increased share of the passenger transport industry. Although battered and bruised, as before, VIA refused to die and pressed onward.

Dome-observation *Kootenay Park* trails an unusual consist of six Skyline dome cars bordered on each end by a single HEP-2 coach. Heading east from Golden to Banff, VIA F40PH-2 No. 6444 leads this special train past Castle Mountain on April 23, 1998, as part of a fiftieth anniversary promotion for one of Japan's leading tour operators, Hankyu Express International. Castle Mountain has long been a prominent landmark in travel posters for the Rocky Mountain parks. *Robert Sandusky*

In 2001, VIA contracted Industrial Rail Services of Moncton, New Brunswick, to rebuild its six remaining Budd cars. Now sporting a simpler livery, refurbished RDC-1s 6148 and 6135 are ready to head south from Courtenay to Victoria over the Esquimalt & Nanaimo Railway. A CP subsidiary until 1999, E&N passed through the hands of several companies until July 1, 2006, when the Southern Railway of British Columbia, a subsidiary of the Washington Marine Group, acquired the line. *Pierre Ozorák*

CHAPTER SIX

Into the New Millennium: *1990–2007*

As historians inform and educate through the written word, statisticians share information through graphs and trends. Graphing the changes in ridership, passenger miles, and VIA's operating ratio of revenues and expenses yields a diagram that mirrors the story told thus far. From its inception as a marketing strategy through the development of VIA as a Crown corporation, the service cuts of 1981, and

Underneath a weather condition known as the Chinook Arch, the eastbound *Canadian* passes through Indus, Alberta, on December 10, 1988. *Richard Yaremko*

the subsequent efforts of front-line staff, maintenance workers, and others to recover, only to be thwarted with a second round of cuts in 1990, the graph's lines would peak and valley accordingly. However, despite significantly lower values after January 15, 1990, the trend that followed was far less turbulent and quite positive. The plotted lines for ridership and passenger miles steadily increased by one-third, driving a rise in revenue, while VIA continued to cut operating costs. The result was a ratio of revenue to expenses that more than doubled to a high of 62.4 percent in 2005. This dramatic turnaround was not the direct result of subsidy reduction. The cuts to service were merely a catalyst for change and throughout the 1990s, VIA would transform its corporate culture, its approach to the passenger train, and even its fleet in order to improve the efficiency of passenger operations.

Hyndman Commission and Reformation

Royal commissions on transportation are a fixture of railroading in Canada, convened every five years on average. However, the Hyndman Commission on National Passenger Transportation was the first to specifically target the issue of passenger travel in all of its modes. Announced in April 1989, the tenure of the commission eclipsed the forthcoming service cuts and included them in their findings published in 1992, contributing to government's further reduction of VIA's subsidy.

The commission concluded that government should no longer "own, finance, maintain or operate Canada's transportation system" and that all modes should be "supported by travelers and not by taxpayers." With this came the recommendation for the withdrawal of government transportation subsidies and limiting government's role in transportation to policymaking. Before losing to the Liberals in the 1993 federal election, the Mulroney government heeded the commission's recommendations and further reduced the VIA Rail subsidy by $100 million.

In response to the funding reduction, a resilient VIA Rail set about accommodating the decrease without eliminating additional services. Understanding the necessity of greater self-sufficiency, VIA restructured its organization to look and function much like a private corporation. Almost every facet of VIA's operations, excluding its trains, was subject to cutbacks during this reformation. The VIA maintenance center in Halifax closed its doors to consolidate the upkeep of eastern transcontinental equipment in Montréal. Some 800 management and administrative positions were eliminated through a corporate reorganization that included the merging of traditionally separate departments such as customer service and transportation. Much to the disappointment of railway enthusiasts, VIA even did away with conductors, resulting in the loss of 252 jobs. A small cadre of service managers who commanded lower wages than the conductors replaced that time-honored position. The net savings in salaries allowed VIA to augment onboard service personnel while realizing savings of $15 million annually in operating costs.

To diminish the impact of the numerous job cuts on its remaining employees, VIA attempted to engage these employees in the restructuring process as a means of acknowledging their value to the organization. The Ideas in Motion program capitalized on worker suggestions to breathe new life into

Heavy snowflakes fall to the ground on Christmas Day 1989 as VIA train No. 1 passes the station mile sign for Stittsville, Ontario, on CP's Carleton Place Subdivision. Following the discontinuance of the *Canadian* 21 days later, CP Rail abandoned this trackage and the rails were later removed. ***A. Ross Harrison***

the employee-depleted company and solicited countless cost-saving and revenue-generating ideas from teams of VIA personnel nationwide.

Hard work avoided further service reductions through corporate restructuring; neither the Mulroney government nor the consecutive Liberal government handed down any decisions to eliminate trains. A decision by CP, however, would affect the continuance of one VIA train. CP Rail had for some time been losing money on freight operations over its "Short Line" that ran from Montréal to Saint John, New Brunswick, through the state of Maine, and

With scarcely a year of operation left, the CP-routed *Canadian* makes its regular daily departure from Toronto on January 21, 1989. With F40PH-2 No. 6426 leading, the train is just passing Jarvis Street. The squirrel-tail of steam trailing from the impressive *Evangeline Park* calls attention to the steam generator car up front, still providing old-style heat for the train. *Robert Sandusky*

in 1993 it made an application to the Canadian Transportation Agency that consented to the abandonment of all CP lines east of Lennoxville, Québec.

Hoping to find a purchaser to operate the line in CP's stead, the government set the abandonment date for January 1, 1995. As the deadline approached, no sales commitments were made and abandonment appeared the most likely scenario. It became apparent to VIA administration that its tri-weekly *Atlantic*, which ran on the Short Line, would have to be canceled. To minimize the impact of this decrease in services to the Maritimes, VIA transferred the *Atlantic*'s equipment to the *Ocean* and increased that train's schedule to six days per week. *The Atlantic*, on its overnight run from Montréal en route for Halifax, arrived in Saint John, New Brunswick, for the last time on the morning of December 16, 1994, ending a 138-year tradition of passenger service to Saint John. The Short Line trackage was eventually parceled out to three railways in a series of last-minute deals that concluded in early January 1995.

Despite all that had transpired to reduce VIA in the years following the 1990 cuts, the bus industry, led once more by Voyageur, rekindled their attack against VIA in 1993 by launching another complaint to the CTA in response to VIA's offering of discounted fares in the Corridor. The same tired argument of unfair advantage was leveled by Voyageur, despite the fact it now offered more than 40 departures per day between Ottawa and Montréal compared to VIA's 14. For the first time in VIA's battles to stave off elimination by the bus companies, the CTA decided in VIA's favor, stating that its pricing initiative did not disadvantage the bus business.

Modernizing the Fleet

Perhaps the most significant project that VIA undertook during its transition phase was the modernization and refurbishment of its fleet. From operational and business management perspectives, electrically heated trains heralded the wave of the future for VIA, being less maintenance-intensive and less expensive to operate compared to their steam-heated counterparts. Anticipation of the Head End Power (HEP) refurbishment program was clearly in the minds of VIA planners when

The quiet at a level crossing in the St. Lawrence Valley near Lemieux, Québec, is briefly interrupted when VIA RDC-2 No. 6225 rushes by with an RDC-1 in tow. *Le Champlain* in name only, these two Budd cars are the September 27, 1987, equivalent of the smart little five-car *Champlain* that the CN purchased from the Reading and once ran on this route. *Pierre Fournier*

the first HEP-equipped F40PH-2 locomotives were acquired in the mid-1980s to replace VIA's aging fleet of steam generator–equipped cab units.

Although testing of leased Amtrak *Superliner* equipment in Canada had been successful, the federal government determined that the cost of new equipment far exceeded what they wished to spend on the replacement of rolling stock. But they did comprehend the advantages of mechanically heated and air-conditioned passenger cars. Instead of procuring new cars, plans to refurbish a portion of VIA's existing fleet were formally announced on May 19, 1987. Applications were tendered for a rebuild of passenger cars

A ticket cover for passengers traveling "Silver and Blue" class aboard the *Canadian* between Toronto and Vancouver. *Author collection*

from the transcontinental fleet to modernize their interiors and upgrade their outdated steam-heating systems with electrical systems. Ultimately, CN was awarded a contract to rebuild 151 ex-CPR stainless-steel cars plus six other stainless-steel cars acquired from U.S. railroads during the mid-1980s. Originally, VIA intended to include 33 non-stainless-steel ex-CN baggage cars and coaches in the rebuild program, but an inspection of this equipment revealed significant structural deterioration that was too costly to remedy. To supplement this loss, VIA went shopping for passenger cars south of the border just as Pierre Delagrave had done some three decades previous.

VIA acquired its first lot of second-hand equipment in 1987 with the purchase of four dome coaches from various American railways. VIA also bartered 18 *Tempo* cars with the Denver, Rio Grande & Western railroad for a dome coach and a dome observation car that, interestingly enough, were originally built for the *California Zephyr*, the same train so admired by Buck Crump that originally inspired the purchase of stainless-steel equipment for *The Canadian*.

The second lot of 30 cars included 2 domes, 18 coaches, and 10 baggage cars obtained between 1988 and 1991. These cars added an additional flavor of American railroad heritage to the VIA Rail roster, coming from such roads as the Pennsylvania, New York Central, and the Rock Island. CN refused to renovate this second group of equipment for the price negotiated in the original agreement, so VIA retendered the contract to Septa Rail of Montréal.

The first cars selected for overhaul entered CN's Pointe St-Charles shops in 1987 and it was anticipated that delivery of the refurbished cars to VIA would commence in mid-1989. Delays pushed the completion forward to the following summer and rising program costs were mitigated by VIA's choice to perform engineering and design services internally rather than contracting them out. Logistics savings were also made through in-house management of procurement and inventory control of all material required, ranging from carpets to air-conditioning units.

The scope of the HEP program was reduced following the service cuts of January 1990, and 15 cars, including the 4 dome observation cars and all 7 secondhand dome cars, were removed from the refurbishment list. Those no longer slated for rebuild were placed in storage. The last overhauled car rolled out of the shops in June 1994, concluding a project that saved VIA some $20

VIA FPA-4 No. 6791 makes a station stop in Smiths Falls, Ontario, in September 1983. Today, VIA owns trackage north of this location through to Ottawa and operates its Ottawa–Brockville–Toronto trains on CP trackage between Smiths Falls and Brockville. *Author collection*

million in operating costs by enabling faster schedules with less en route servicing.

The new fleet was unveiled mid-program, providing an aura of encouragement for the railway in a year that was otherwise rather devastating. The public first caught a glimpse of the complete stainless-steel consist in May 1990 at a gala ceremony called "Of Style and Steel," an immediate success with railfans and travelers alike. A new standard of onboard first-class service was also introduced with the "Silver and Blue" class aboard the reintroduced *Canadian*, which now served the route of the former *Super Continental*. As icing on the cake, the HEP program earned VIA the prestigious Brunel Award for outstanding visual design in railway transportation, a fitting distinction for such an ambitious project.

The complement of rebuilt stainless-steel equipment was sufficient for VIA's long-haul needs following the 1990 service reductions, and increasing numbers of steam-heated equipment were shunted into

Alternating equipment for this route with Amtrak, on October 21, 1990, it is VIA's turn to provide motive power and rolling stock for train 181, the *International*. VIA F40PH-2 No. 6444 hauls a six-car consist of LRC-1 coaches. Of a larger set formerly leased by Amtrak for evaluation of LRC stock, VIA refurbished eight LRC-1 cars for exclusive use on this route from 1988 to 1994. Following the discontinuance of the *International* 10 years later, VIA and Amtrak continue to jointly operate the *Maple Leaf*, while Amtrak runs two other services to Canada: the *Amtrak Cascades* between Seattle and Vancouver and the *Adirondack* from New York to Montréal. *Andreas Kellar*

deadlines. Once the mainstay of CN and VIA fleets, the blue and yellow–liveried equipment was fast disappearing from VIA trains throughout Canada.

Improvements in the Corridor

Wanting to augment and improve services in the Corridor, VIA examined the possibility of another reconditioning arrangement similar to the HEP program. After 10 years of service, the LRC equipment was well-used and also needed refurbishment. Elsewhere, the remaining steam-heated equipment that served southern Ontario, northern Manitoba, and northern Québec was overdue for retirement.

Starting with its fleet of LRCs, VIA unveiled a new look for their Corridor equipment in June 1991 and initiated a renovation program to apply an improved interior design to its 100 LRC cars; 75 were reconfigured as 74-seat coaches and the remaining 25 as 56-seat VIA-1 first class cars. VIA also retired a small group of LRC-1 coaches that were part of a larger complement

9175
CN
9175

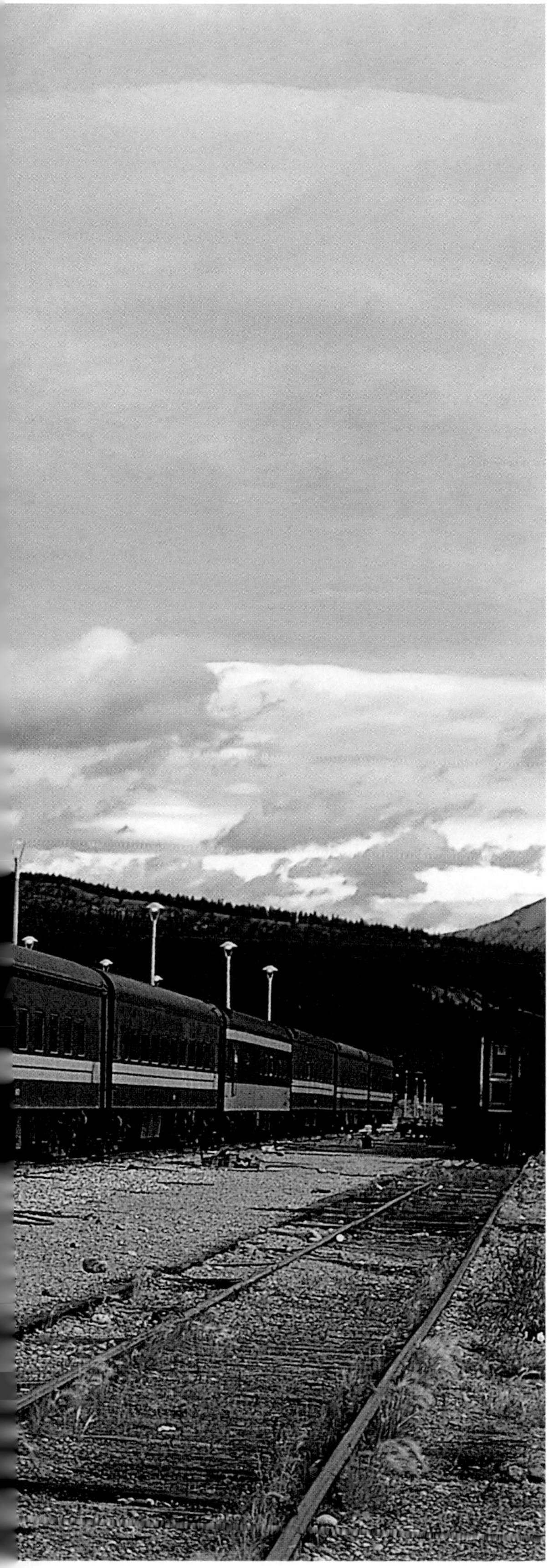

previously leased to Amtrak in 1981 and 1982. Upon contract expiration, Amtrak declined an option to purchase the 10 cars and 2 locomotives it had been testing; the entire consist was returned to VIA, who in 1988 refurbished 8 of the coaches for dedicated service on its *International* between Toronto, Sarnia, and Chicago. The entire LRC refurbishment program was completed in 1994.

To address the replacement issue for the small number of steam-heated equipment that lingered on the roster, and to increase capacity within the Corridor, VIA went shopping once more for used passenger equipment and purchased 33 Budd-built stainless-steel cars from various U.S. railroads. Dubbed the "HEP-2 Program," each car was overhauled and, although similar to long-haul coaches on the outside, the interiors closely matched those of the refurbished LRCs.

VIA held a ceremony to unveil its new batch of reborn equipment, placing a three-car HEP-2 train on display at Toronto's Union Station on February 29, 1996. The festivities also introduced VIA's new uniforms for front-line staff and customer service personnel throughout the Corridor.

VIA's conversion to electrically heated, stainless-steel HEP cars on its transcontinental trains and in the Corridor was complete. When the final HEP-2 coach was delivered in March 1996, the remaining three pockets of steam-heated equipment in northern Manitoba, northern Québec, and southwestern Ontario was on borrowed time.

As a final encore for the blue and yellow equipment once used in transcontinental service, two ex-CN 80-seat coaches were recommissioned and united with a specially painted F40PH-2 locomotive for use in the "Rediscover Canada with VIA Rail" sweepstakes, jointly sponsored by VIA Rail, Home Hardware, and the Canadian Tourism Commission. In a related public lottery, 20 fortunate couples were awarded a cross Canada

On one of her last assignments before retirement, Canadian National F7Au No. 9175 is set to lead the *Skeena* from Jasper, Alberta, to Prince Rupert, British Columbia, on September 5, 1979. Built for hauling freight, 9175 lacks steam-generating equipment, hence the need for a purpose-built car cut in between the passenger consist and the locomotive. ***D. L. Zeutschel photo, author collection***

rail tour between Prince Rupert and Halifax on this vintage train.

End of Steam Heat in Northern Canada

Declared an "essential service" by the federal government, the *Hudson Bay* in northern Manitoba and the *Abitibi* in northern Québec, with their all-blue-and-yellow consists, were spared from discontinuation in 1990. Because these northern routes are tertiary components of the national passenger network compared to the profitable Corridor and more popular transcontinental routes, they were among the last areas targeted for conversion to HEP.

The cancellation of *The Atlantic* in December 1994 freed up three train sets of HEP equipment. This sudden surplus of overhauled passenger cars allowed for the provision of better-conditioned stock on the two northern routes. Delivery and integration of *The Atlantic*'s cars on the scheduled runs of the *Hudson Bay* and the *Abitibi* began early in 1995 as newly refurbished HEP baggage cars, coaches, and diners were transferred to Montréal and Winnipeg. Crews of both trains familiarized themselves with the

In recent years, VIA has become known for the interesting liveries applied to several of its locomotives, especially those assigned to the Corridor. Here, VIA F40PH-2 No. 6429 is decorated in a Telus Mobility-Vancouver 2010 Winter Olympics color scheme as she pauses with train 75 at Brampton on June 22, 2003. *Pierre Ozorák*

In her third year of VIA service, P42DC No. 902 showcases VIA's joint-train operations on December 10, 2003. Passing the hamlet of Mallorytown, Ontario, the unified consist will soon arrive in Brockville and part company, with the 902 heading north for Smiths Falls and Ottawa, and F40PH-2 No. 6438 continuing on to Montréal. *Bob Heathorn, Ian McCord collection*

new equipment throughout the delivery process as the services and accommodations on the Budd-built fleet differed slightly from what had been available on the older steam-heated equipment. A single Budd-built dining car was placed on a siding at Winnipeg's Union Station and used as an instructional car for meal-service personnel throughout the summer and fall of 1995. Slowly but surely, the all-HEP train sets were placed into the equipment rotation cycle, replacing older steam-heated consists. Before long, queues of blue and yellow passenger cars at both the Montréal and Winnipeg maintenance centers lengthened as the ex-CN equipment was removed from service.

On April 26, 1996, the era of steam-heated passenger equipment in northern Canada came to a close when the last all-blue-and-yellow-equipped *Abitibi* arrived in Montréal from northern Québec. The ex-CN carbon-steel train set was sent back to the yards where it was shunted into the dead line after only a cursory cleaning of its interior. With the replacement of steam with electric heat complete on VIA's northern routes, yard

VIA Rail Canada

IMPORTANT
Subject to conditions of
contract on back.
Sous réserve des conditions
du contrat figurant au vers...

Domed Park Car • Transcontinental trains *Voiture panoramique Parc • Trains transcontinentaux*

VIA ceased the use of ticket sleeves in favor of a single-sheet, fold-over stub. This cover was issued during the summer of 1995. *Author collection*

and station heating supply lines became redundant and steam flows at both the Winnipeg and Montréal maintenance centers were disconnected; no more would latent wisps of white vapor be seen rising above VIA's railyards.

Changes to the scheduling and accommodations available on northern routes were effected once the transition to HEP was complete. Passengers aboard the *Hudson Bay* between Winnipeg and Churchill would continue to enjoy sleeping car service while those aboard the Montréal–Sennetaire *Abitibi* would not. The HEP equivalent of the ex-CN E series sleeping cars formerly used on both routes was only provided for the *Hudson Bay*. Without sleeping car service, the *Abitibi* was rescheduled for daytime operation. Further schedule changes to the all-daylight service in northern Québec came later that spring in the form of simultaneous operations. In a measure to further cut costs, the *Abitibi* departed northbound with the Montréal–Jonquière train and coupled with the *Saguenay* between Montréal and Hervey, Québec, running jointly for a portion of the journey.

The Last of Many

Equipment troubles with the HEP-1 cars and F40PH locomotives developed during the fall and winter of 1997–1998, causing numerous difficulties for the railway. As the previous winter was more temperate, the burden placed on the electric heating systems of the HEP fleet was light and problems from extreme temperature loads were not immediately apparent. As a result, the frequent heating system breakdowns that occurred as the temperature nosedived were quite unexpected.

The acute cold of a Manitoba winter defied the ability of the heating mechanisms on the HEP equipment to sustain adequate climate control, forcing them to draw copious amounts of power from the F40PH-2 locomotives that had replaced the FP9ARM units not 10 months prior. The locomotives themselves began to suffer from the cold and no longer ran efficiently. The net effect was that the entire train would freeze up en route.

The challenges experienced in northern Manitoba were compounded by positive developments for VIA in the Corridor; increased ticket sales and sold-out trains had the unusual complication of magnifying the requirement

VIA has tested a wide variety of equipment for potential use in several of its markets. The ADtranz Flexliner IC3, seen here in Ottawa on September 29, 1996, was evaluated for a two-month period. Other test initiatives have included a BREL Railbus in northern Manitoba in 1986–1987 and the Bombardier Jet Train in 2002. To date, none of the abovementioned equipment has been purchased by VIA. *Pierre Ozorák*

for serviceable motive power across the entire network. Until modifications could be made to the F40s, and pending the acquisition of new locomotives, a temporary solution was required for the heating problems.

Seven FP9ARM locomotives were selected from the dead lines to be equipped with an HEP generator and quickly pressed back into service on both the *Hudson Bay* and the *Abitibi* to free up the F40s for Corridor service. These F units remained on the active roster into the new millennium, when the arrival of 21 General Electric P42DC Genesis locomotives in 2001 gave VIA enough breathing room with its motive power fleet to properly winterize several F40PH-2s, forcing a second retirement of 6 of the 7 FP9s.

Only one F unit currently remains listed on the VIA Rail roster: FP9ARM 6300, the last of many, steadfastly soldiers on at

Attached to a conventional steam-heat consist, LRC-3 No. 6924 requires the assistance of a steam generator. Accelerating past the platform, the short train coats the stone station at Napanee, Ontario, in a dusting of snow. *Coo/West collection*

the Vancouver maintenance center. No longer plying the rails in revenue service, the dignified 6300 maintains her usefulness as an occasional shop switcher and a definite railfan favorite lovingly cared for by maintenance center staff.

A Renaissance of Rail Travel

Of all government officials since the inception of VIA, perhaps only David Collenette matched the dedicated concern once shown by Otto Lang for passenger rail. Appointed to the post of transport minister in 1997, Collenette would come to the aid of VIA by increasing funding for the first time in half a decade, thereby ensuring the success of the railway into the new millennium.

In the years following the 1992 subsidy reduction, VIA made a concerted effort to reduce this operating subsidy even further through restructuring efforts and continued cost reductions, reaching an all-time low of $163 million in 2001. By this point, ideas for continuing to provide the highest level of service possible while reducing costs were almost exhausted. Fortunately, Collenette had an idea of his own.

In February 1998, Collenette approached the House of Commons' Standing Committee on Transport (SCOT) to review the status of

Overnight service between Montréal and Toronto was reinstated in 2000 with the inauguration of train 50/51, the *Enterprise*. This service was reequipped with newer *Renaissance* cars in 2002. For scheduling reasons, the westbound *Enterprise* is taking an hour-long pause in Kingston at around 2:30 a.m., and will continue on to Toronto two hours later. *Tim Reid*

rail passenger services and formulate suggestions to further assist VIA. SCOT released its report, "The Renaissance of Passenger Rail in Canada," five months later, concluding that what VIA had achieved and maintained with its then-current level of resources was no longer sustainable. Among its recommendations favoring "private-public partnerships" to solve VIA's equipment and infrastructure needs, was a call for a 10-year funding package from government for VIA to renegotiate track access in the Corridor with the freight railways and for government to confer commercial Crown corporation status on VIA to provide it with greater access to private capital—because VIA was not permitted to borrow money and had to rely on government appropriations as its sole source of capital funding. SCOT also encouraged a closer examination of high-speed rail proposals, two of which were made in the late 1990s. The Ontario-Québec Rapid Train Task Force, jointly commissioned by the Ontario and Québec governments, concluded in its report that high-speed service within the Corridor was feasible but would require a large amount of government funding. Private interests put forth the other plan and modeled it after the Florida Overland eXpress (FOX) consortium that had at one time proposed the construction of a high-speed link between

2684N
902
VIA
VIA Rail Canada

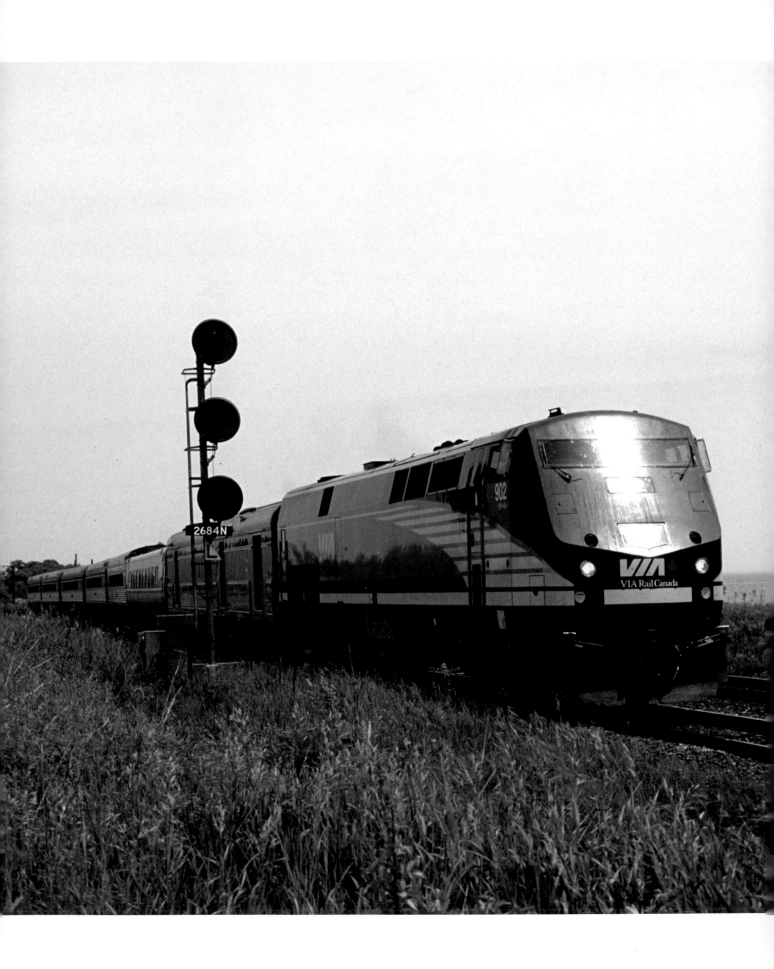

Miami, Orlando, and Tampa, Florida. The Canadian version, called LYNX, surmised that private industry could build and finance, with some government assistance, a 200-mile-per-hour (322-kilometer-per-hour) passenger train between Québec City, Montréal, Ottawa, and Toronto.

The response from government to the SCOT report in October 1998 included a 10-year commitment to provide stable funding capped at $170 million per annum and allowed for VIA to develop a 10-year strategic plan with Transport Canada to continue revitalizing rail passenger service. The high-speed service concept proved once more to be far too adventurous for government and was shelved in favor of the status quo. Two years later, Collenette announced an additional subsidy package worth $401.9 million in capital funding, and with this pledge VIA embarked once more on a project to renew its fleet, this time purchasing new equipment.

VIA Rail's "Renaissance of Rail Travel," as it would become known, began with the arrival of three Nightstar passenger cars from England in June 2000 for a series of tests. This equipment, once destined for use in the Channel Tunnel, was part of a program to run sleeping cars between Britain and the European continent. Delays and cost overruns resulted in the cancellation of the Nightstar, and the 139 cars, most with unfinished interiors, were placed into storage. Trials began in earnest during November 2000 with a P42DC Genesis locomotive leased from Amtrak for two days of high-speed tests east of Montréal, and continued between Montréal and Ottawa with an LRC locomotive in the lead, successfully concluding the evaluation by the end of that month.

On December 15, 2000, Collenette, alongside VIA officials, announced the purchase of all 139 Nightstar passenger cars, much to the delight of Transport 2000 President Harry Gow, who stated that the acquisition was "a genuine bargain for Canada's

A single LRC coach to provide VIA-1 first-class service stands out amid the stainless-steel consist of train 57. P42DC No. 902, skirting Lake Ontario, has only a few miles to go before passing Port Hope with the *La Salle* on June 21, 2005. The appearance of P42DC motive power has given most VIA trains a more aesthetic appearance, blending in with almost anything that is coupled behind them. Soon even the F40PH-2s will be restyled with similar color schemes. ***Robert Sandusky***

Prior to crossing the Victoria Bridge to the island of Montréal, the conductor of VIA train 11, the *Atlantic*, exchanges waves with the engineer aboard an eastbound CN freight at St-Lambert. *A. Ross Harrison*

passenger railway." Destined for service on the *Ocean* and within the Corridor between Montréal and Québec City, the cars would be overhauled and aptly rechristened as Renaissance equipment.

In addition to the P42 locomotive from Amtrak, VIA had also leased an F59PHI locomotive from Sound Transit in Seattle for evaluation during the summer months of 2000. VIA examined each locomotive and eventually ordered 21 Genesis units from General Electric in April 2001 with delivery beginning six months later. The arrival of these new units brought about the retirement of the last seven LRC locomotives from the VIA roster. As it was, the majority of LRC motive power, prone to electrical failure, had been in storage since 1995. By 2001 the few that remained in operation had surpassed their expected 15-year service life and were due for replacement. Also included in the Renaissance of Rail Travel program was the upgrade of station facilities, first within the Corridor and then across Canada, and the refurbishment of the six remaining RDCs on the VIA roster, assigned

The racing waters of the Kicking Horse River are only a few feet away from the eastbound *Canadian*, snaking its way toward Glenogle, British Columbia, on June 14, 1987. *Ted Ellis*

to the Sudbury–White River route in northern Ontario and the *Malahat* on Vancouver Island between Victoria and Courtney.

More recently, VIA was also able to update the plant and signaling equipment on rail infrastructure it had acquired from CN and CP following two abandonment requests made by these railways to the CTA in the 1990s. To prevent another occurrence like the 1994 cancellation of *The Atlantic*, VIA opted to purchase the two lines slated for abandonment in order to maintain service. For the first time in its history, VIA became a bona fide railway in the truest sense of the word—it owned its own rail and rights-of-way: 34.5 miles (56 kilometers) of CP's Smiths Falls Subdivision from Smiths Falls, Ontario, north to Ottawa, and 65.2 miles (105 kilometers) of CN's Alexandria Subdivision between Ottawa and Glen Robertson, Ontario (99.7 miles [161 kilometers] in all). The remainder of its services are operated on the rails of other companies under negotiated trackage rights.

The Constant of Politics

In 2007, VIA continues to operate almost 500 trains weekly on some 7,700 miles (12,392 kilometers) of track. The past 15 years have by far been the most stable for VIA, and the railway continues its trend of slow growth, still at risk of political whim. Since 2000, Canadian politics have been incredibly turbulent with three elections and as many prime ministers in six years. Each change in administration and leadership was

To give students a break on travel expenses, the VIA "6 Pak" offers holders of a valid International Student Identity Card the opportunity to save almost 50 percent off a regular one-way fare by purchasing three roundtrip tickets between the same two stations. VIA also offers a similar program for business travelers called "Biz Pak." *Author collection*

yet another opportunity for politicians to drag out the VIA Rail football and punt it around Parliament Hill, resulting in several unsuccessful attempts to legislate the future of VIA Rail.

David Collenette tabled yet another version of a VIA Rail Canada Act in 2003. Bill C-26 has been the most successful of all in that it received a second reading before the House of Commons, only to be prorogued following the resignation of Prime Minister Jean Chrétien after 10 years in office. Prior to stepping down, Chrétien announced a generous $700 million capital funding package for VIA over a five-year period. Regrettably for VIA, intense acri-

In June 2002, VIA reequipped its overnight *Enterprise*, trains 50 and 51, with new, European-style Renaissance stock from England. Montréal-bound 50 cruises through the suburb of Pointe Claire on the morning of September 17, 2002. Overnight service in the Corridor lasted until September 2005. The yellow box atop 6425's cab is an air-conditioning unit, installed during the late 1990s for the comfort of the engineers. *Robert Sandusky*

mony between Chrétien and his successor, Paul Martin, the former Canada Steamship Lines president who had so vehemently argued against VIA Rail subsidies from the late 1970s into the early 1990s, resulted in the subsidy's immediate cancellation.

Leading a Liberal government rocked by scandal and rumors of scandal, Martin was forced to call an election shortly after assuming power. Remarkably, the Liberals were reelected in June 2004, albeit with a very unstable minority government. Nevertheless, once the House of Commons reconvened, the VRCA previously proposed by Collenette was retabled as Bill C-44. Yet again, it was prorogued when the Martin government fell

After 101 gorgeous miles (163 kilometers) from Sydney through scenic Cape Breton Island, VIA's *Bras D'Or* makes a stop at Port Hawkesbury to change crews prior to crossing the Canso Causeway that links the island to mainland Nova Scotia on August 29, 2001. The Sydney–Port Hawkesbury portion of the trip is by far the most stunning, but almost 200 miles (322 kilometers)are left and passengers will enjoy onboard entertainment from Tourism Nova Scotia staff who showcase Maritime artistry, dance, and song. *Pierre Ozorák*

18 months later, forcing another election in which the Liberals would relinquish power to the Conservatives, this time under Stephen Harper. The bill that had contained the VIA Rail Canada Act was retabled in 2006, but the VRCA was removed. As of early 2007, another attempt to legislate a secure mandate for VIA had yet to be made.

Via VIA

As always, VIA presses on and continues to improve its core services and to utilize ingenuity in customer service. Perks such as wireless internet for business travelers, the "VIA Preference" points program, and competitive "Flexifare" rates, as well as excellent onboard and station service, timely schedules, comfortable accommodations, and a superior safety record keep customers coming back to the rails year after year. For many Canadians and tourists alike, VIA Rail has become the preferred way to travel.

Fleet maintenance continues to be a priority for the railway, which commenced two pilot programs in 2006. As part of a midlife rebuild program, F40PH-2 No. 6400 was sent to the Canada Allied Diesel shops of Lachine, Québec. Delivered in December 2006, it is the

In preparation for departure from the former CN station in Vancouver, the engineer aboard VIA FP9A No. 6550 has opened the blow-down valves on his locomotive's Vapor Clarkson steam generator, shooting a plume of steam into the air. A standard operating procedure, this interesting display lasts only a few seconds. Once complete, the crew will complete its checks and await word from the conductor before heading east through the Rocky Mountains. *Jim Shepard photo, author collection*

first of 53 units of this type to be re-shopped to extend the fleet service life by an estimated 15 years. A plan to refurbish the LRC coaches by VIA at their Montréal maintenance center has also been submitted to government. If both programs receive approval and government funding, VIA expects to overhaul 25 LRC cars per year over four years, along with the bulk of the F40PH-2 fleet.

VIA courted the tourist train concept again in 2001 with the *Bras D'Or*, a daylight service that was a tremendous success with patrons who enjoyed the beautiful scenery of Cape Breton Island from two dome cars included on the consist. The train ran during the summer months on CN trackage from Halifax to Truro and on to Sydney, Nova Scotia, over the CN's former Hopewell and

Lacking a single VIA Rail locomotive due to equipment shortages, CP Rail motive power saves the day. A trio of high-hood, passenger-service GP9s led by 8515 bring the *Canadian* into Field, British Columbia, on July 25, 1981. *J. M. Seidl*

Sydney subdivisions, sold to RailAmerica in 1993 and operated by their Cape Breton & Central Nova Scotia Railway (CB&CNS) subsidiary. The *raison d'être* for this short line railroad disappeared with the closure of the coal-producing Prince Mine in 2001, but its operation was protracted by the need to ship out a large latent supply of previously extracted coal; once complete, the line would close. With abandonment a likely possibility, VIA opted to cancel the *Bras D'Or* tourist service. However, this discontinuance could merely be temporary as Xstrata, a Swiss mining company, won a bid to reopen the Donkin coal mine in late 2005. Higher commodity prices combined with a $10 million subsidy from the Nova Scotia provincial government to the CB&CNS to maintain the line for at least five years may see VIA reinstate the *Bras D'Or* during the summer of 2007.

Since its inception, VIA has always been a steward of the community and has encouraged its employees to involve themselves and volunteer for myriad programs. From annual support for the United Way to the gathering of donations for victims of the 1985 Barrie tornado to a contract to sell only fair trade coffee aboard its trains, VIA excels with its

VIA RDC-1 No. 6127 in the hallowed space of the Spadina roundhouse after her latest assignment. In the late hours of a March evening in 1985, a lone shop worker briskly goes about his business at the end of 6127's stall, washing off the dirt and grime accumulated from many miles of service. *Andreas Kellar*

corporate compassion. Perhaps the most poignant examples are the 2005 Veteran's Train and the War Bride's Train the following year

Given that every year fewer surviving Korean War and World War II veterans would have the chance to attend the national Remembrance Day service in Ottawa, VIA ticket agents Ron Jackson and Peggy Topple conceived the idea to send a few local veterans from Halifax aboard the *Ocean* to attend the national ceremony as part of 2005 "Year of the Veteran" celebrations. Their idea caught on and ballooned into a 30-car train that would see veterans from all armed services boarding at towns along the route. When the *Ocean* reached Montréal, more than 350 war veterans and their families from the Maritimes changed trains for Ottawa and arrived in time for the November 11 ceremony. VIA staff even had the presence of mind to include the rank, service history, and accomplishments of every soldier on their manifest for posterity and thus provide an extra degree of personalized attention. So goes travel on VIA, with a dedicated spirit and quiet dignity befitting the Canadian nation and the train-loving people it serves.

EPILOGUE

The last book to cover the VIA Rail story was completed in 1982 by Tom Nelligan, who at the time concluded that the future of the five-year-old railway was somewhat uncertain but held a marked level of promise. After the first round of cuts in 1981, few could have predicted what was to come by decade's end.

The events of September 11, 2001, and subsequent threats to airplane security have irreversibly changed how the airline industry operates. Ever-increasing safety measures at airports continue to prolong the boarding process for aircraft to such a degree that the time required for travel between Ottawa and downtown Toronto by air and rail is almost

After pulling the cut-bar and opening up the coupler, the conductor gives the signal and watches carefully as the engineer backs up the train from the left side of the frame to couple both cars together. Next, both conductor and porter will connect the steam and brake lines and ensure all is in good order before departure. *Coo/West collection*

equitable. Travel habits of passengers within the Corridor are changing and VIA's future appears to be more promising than ever.

Stable funding established for VIA in the late 1990s has fostered an atmosphere for sustainable growth and, as a result, VIA continues to innovate and expand. Starting on August 15, 2006, VIA offered a series of commuter passes for its intercity trains that operate outside the purview of commuter trains run by GO Transit in Toronto and AMT in Montréal. Plans to implement high-speed rail in both the Edmonton–Calgary and Québec City–Windsor corridors, both long purported as viable high-speed routes, remain on the table. The reestablishment of certain routes lost in the 1990 cuts are also rumored to be underway and could result in portions of Canadian Pacific's main line between Winnipeg, Calgary, and Vancouver seeing a return of rail service.

Irrespective of these improvements, a pressing need remains for the legislation of a VIA Rail Canada Act to ensure the long-term sustainability of the railway. Rail passenger service cannot operate entirely without some form of government subsidy and every major industrialized nation funds its passenger railways to one degree or another. Canada is by no means immune to this necessity and in order to maintain VIA, a clear and concise mandate is required to clarify its funding and costing requirements and define VIA's role with government and the railways. Until such time as this becomes a reality, VIA Rail will undoubtedly stay the course that it adopted during the mid-1990s that has thus far proved beneficial.

French railway engineer Louis Armand once envisaged that if passenger trains could only survive the twentieth century, their success in the new millennium was assured. Almost three decades have lapsed since VIA's inception and in the face of unfavorable odds, VIA succeeded in crossing the millennial threshold. With continuing support and commitment from government, taxpayers, and travelers alike, rail passenger service from VIA Rail is poised to thrive in Canada for many years to come.

Reminiscent of a scene in the Rockies, VIA train 603, the *Abitibi*, exits a tunnel north of Fitzpatrick, Québec, on CN's Saint-Maurice Subdivision in July 2005. ***George Pitarys***

Sources

Books

Anderson, G. W. *Canadian Pacific's Trans-Canada Limited (1919–1930)*. Calgary, Alta.: British Railway Modellers of North America, 1990.

Bunting, P. M. *Changing Trains: A Commercially Sustainable Railway Passenger Policy for Canada*. Kingston, Ont.: P. M. Bunting & Assoc., 1998.

Bunting, P. M., and Everett Johnson. *Western Transcontinental Railway Passenger Service: Market Opportunities and Requirements for Modernization*. Calgary, Alta.: Everett Johnston and Assoc. Ltd., 1984.

Cruise, D., and A. Griffiths. *Lords of the Line*. Toronto: Viking Books, 1988.

Dorin, P. C. *The Canadian National Railways Story*. Seattle, Wash.: Superior Publishing Co., 1975.

Garden, J. F. *Nicholas Morant's Canadian Pacific*. Revelstoke, B.C.: Footprint Publishing, 1991.

Holland, K. J. *Rails to the Border: The New York Central, Chesapeake & Ohio and Wabash in Southern Ontario, Vol. 1*. Calgary, Alta.: British Railway Modellers of North America, 2001.

Jackson, Michael. *Proceedings of the First National Rail Passenger Conference 29–31 October 1976*. Regina, Sask.: University of Regina Press, 1977.

Lavallée, Omer, ed. *Canadian Pacific Steam Locomotives*. Toronto: Railfare Enterprises Ltd., 1985.

Lukasiewicz, J. *The Railway Game*. Toronto: McLelland & Stewart, 1976.

McKay, D. *The People's Railway*. Vancouver: Douglas & McIntyre, 1992.

Miller-Barstow, D. H. *Beatty of the C.P.R.* Toronto: McLelland & Stewart, 1951.

Nelligan, Tom. *VIA Rail Canada: The First Five Years*. Park Forest, Ill.: PTJ Publishing, 1982.

Pammett, John H., et al. *The Integration Question*. Toronto: Addison-Wesley, 1984.

Perl, Anthony. *New Departures: Rethinking Rail Passenger Policy in the Twenty-First Century*. Lexington, Ky.: University of Kentucky Press, 2002.

Saunders, Richard. *Main Lines: Rebirth of North American Railroads, 1970–2002*. DeKalb, Ill.: Northern Illinois University Press, 2001.

———. *Merging Lines: American Railroads, 1900–1970*. DeKalb, Ill.: Northern Illinois University Press, 2001.

Steinbrenner, Richard T. *The American Locomotive Company: A Centennial Remembrance*. Warren, N.J.: On Track Publishers, 2003.

Stevenson, Garth, et al. *Privatization, Public Policy and Public Corporations in Canada*. Halifax, N.S.: The Institute for Research on Public Policy, 1988.

Weaver, Kent R. *The Politics of Industrial Change*. Washington, D.C.: Brookings Institution, 1985.

Articles

Angus, Fred. "The Fiftieth Anniversary of Canadian National Railways Lightweight Steel Passenger Fleet." *Canadian Rail* 504 (2005): 11.

———. "The 50th Anniversary of the CPR Stainless Steel Passenger Fleet." *Canadian Rail* 503 (2004): 211.

Brown, James A. "The New Trains." *Upper Canada Railway Society Newsletter* (November 1965): 197–199.

Calgary Herald. Untitled article, February 4, 1976.

Cubukgil, Adil, and Richard M. Soberman. "Costs of Rail Passenger Service in Canada: An Examination of Institutional Problems." *Proceedings – Twenty-fifth Annual Meeting: Transportation Research Forum* 25 no. 4 (1984): 89.

De Poe, Norman. Untitled article. *Saturday Night* magazine, 1976.

Hays, Peter. Untitled article. *Halifax Daily Star*, January 15, 1991.
Howell, Peter. "VIA's Budget Cut as President Fired." *Toronto Star*, May 4, 1989: A1.
Lukasiewicz, J. "Public Policy and Technology: Passenger Rail in Canada as an Issue of Modernization." *Canadian Public Policy* 5 no. 4 (Autumn 1979).
Ottawa Citizen. Untitled article, August 27, 1976.
Perl, Anthony. "North American Intercity Rail Passenger Systems." *Transportation Research Board*, 2000.
Robbie, J. T. "I'm a Believer." *Rail and Transit* 1 no. 4 (May–June 1976): 5.

Government Documents

Baldwin, John R. "The Evolution of Transportation Policy in Canada: A Seminar Paper Presented to the Canadian Transport Commission." Ottawa: CTC, 1977.
Bunting, P. M. "Summary of the Pricing and Subsidy of Air and Rail Passenger Transportation for the Canadian Transport Commission, Report #271." Ottawa: CTC, 1976.
Canadian Motor Coach Association. "The Bus Industry vs. VIA Rail." March 8, 1979.
Canadian Transport Commission annual report. Ottawa: CTC, 1969.
Canadian Transport Commission, Railway Transport Committee. "An Interim Report by the Railway Transport Committee on the Rationalization of Montréal/Toronto–Vancouver Passenger Train Services." Ottawa: CTC, 1971.
Carson, C. F. H., and F. C. S. Evans. "Outline Submission of the Canadian Pacific Railway Company to the Royal Commission on Transportation." Montréal: CPR, 1959.
Dominion Bureau of Statistics. "Railway Transport: Operating and Traffic Statistics, Part 4." Ottawa: DBS, 1967–1970.
Government of Canada, internal memo #4307-07-01, January 28, 1977.
———, cabinet document 37-77MC, January 30, 1977.
———, cabinet documents 360-77CR, 360-77CR(TB), and 360-77MC, August 4, 1977.
House of Commons Standing Committee on Transport and Communications, minutes of proceedings and evidence, no. 2, March 3, 1966: 1,578–1,655.
Liberal Party of Canada. "National Liberal Caucus Report of the Federal Liberal Task Force on VIA Rail." Ottawa: 1989.
MacPherson, S., et al. "Royal Commission on Transportation, Vol. 1." Ottawa: Queen's Printer and Controller of Stationary, 1961.
Marchand, Jean. "An Interim Report on Inter-City Passenger Movement in Canada." Ottawa: Transport Canada, 1975.
———. "Transportation Policy: A Framework for Transportation in Canada." Ottawa: Transport Canada, 1975.
Mazankowski, Don, et al. "The Last Straw: Report of the Task Force on Rail Passenger Service." Ottawa: Progressive Conservative Party of Canada, 1981.
McGuire, Cecilia. "100 Years at the Heart of Transportation: A Centennial Perspective of the Canadian Transport Agency and Its Predecessors." Ottawa: Canadian Transport Agency, 2004.
Minister of Transport. "Acquisition of Passenger Trains." Ottawa: July 14, 1977.
Mozersky, Kenneth A., et al. "Report of the Inquiry into the On-Time Performance of VIA Rail Canada Inc." Hull, P.Q.: Canadian Transport Commission, November 1984.
Statistics Canada. "Railway Transport: Operating and Traffic Statistics, Part 4." Ottawa: Statistics Canada, 1971–1975.
Transport 2000. "Submission to the House of Commons Standing Committee on Transport in the Matter of Planned Service Reductions for VIA." October 1989.
Transport Canada. "Directive for the Guidance of the Canadian Transport Commission on Rail Passenger Services." Ottawa: Transport Canada, January 29, 1976.

———, memo to Treasury Board #3510-2. Ottawa: Transport Canada, n.d.
———, minutes of the Rail Passenger Committee of Transport Canada. Ottawa: Transport Canada, May 27, 1977.
———. "Paper on Outline for Controls of VIA." Ottawa: Transport Canada, September 1977.
———. "The Potential for a Canadian Rail Passenger Program." Ottawa: Transport Canada, 1976.
———, Transport Canada file #S-1022-6-77. Ottawa: Transport Canada, January 26, 1977.
Transport Canada, Railway Transportation Directorate. "Evaluation of Legislative Alternatives for VIA Rail Canada, Part One, Legislative Strategy for VIA Rail Canada." Ottawa: Transport Canada, 1978.
Transport Canada and Interdepartmental Rail Passenger Coordination Committee. "Report to Treasury Board on the Evaluation of Principal Options for the Finance and Corporate Structures of VIA Rail Canada and the Relationship between Government and VIA and VIA and the Railways." Treasury Board file #S3510-2. Ottawa: December 20, 1977.
Transportation Services Branch, Alberta Department of Economic Development. "Rail Passenger Service in the Calgary–Edmonton Corridor: The Government of Alberta's Position." Edmonton, Alta.: April 1985
Treasury Board, document #741167. February 1976.

Other Sources

Bandeen, Robert. Interview with Chris Greenlaw. May 29, 2006.
Canadian National. *CN Public Relations*. Issue #6229, April 23, 1976.
———, internal correspondence, "VIA/CN Rail Charges," July 6, 1978.
———, internal memorandum, May 1, 1980.
———, "Passenger Sales & Service" passenger promotion memo, May 4, 1966.
———. "Reconciliation sheet of passenger car sales," August 1980.
Canadian Pacific. "CPR charges to the Rail Transport Committee Railway Economy Analysis Branch of the Canadian Transport Commission for VIA Rail Services." December 16, 1982.
———, internal memorandum on the details of passenger equipment sales to VIA, May 4, 1977.
Horner, Hugh M., et al. "Rail Passenger Action Force Letter of Transmittal to The Honourable Don Mazankowski, Minister of Transport and the Honourable Benoît Bouchard, Minister of State for Transport." May 23, 1985.
Lang, Otto. Interview with the author. May 29, 2006.
———, letter to Treasury Board President Robert Andras, March 21, 1978.
Lower, Doug and Michel Lebel. "Trains en quête de passagers." Montréal: Radio Canada, June 24, 1984.
Martin, Paul, letter to Otto Lang, March 9, 1979.
———, letter to Otto Lang, December 19, 1978.
Roberts, Frank, letter to Otto Lang, March 7, 1979.
RTC, letter to the CNR, January 27, 1977.
Sainte-Marie, Yves and Gaston Poiré. "La reduction des services de VIA Rail en novembre '81." Montréal: Transport 2000, 1984.
TGO 2000. "Transport Action" (French), Vol. 12, #2/3, July 1990.
Transport 2000. "VIA: A Better Way: The Transport 2000 Counter-plan." Ottawa: July 1989.
VIA Rail Canada, annual reports, 1978–2006.
———. "Summary of the 1993–1997 Corporate Plan and 1993 Operating and Capital"
———. *VIA Ontario Public Affairs Newsletter*. February 28, 1986.
———. Budgets. Montréal: VIA Rail Canada Inc., March 1993.
VIA/CN newsletter. November 1976.

INDEX